The Girl's Guide
to
Manners
(and all that good stuff.)

An imprint of Rose Publishing, Inc.
Carson, CA
www.Rose-Publishing.com

Check out all of the books in
The Girl's Guide Series

The Girl's Guide
to
Manners
(and all that good stuff.)

Tina M. Cho

Dedication

I dedicate this book to my daughter, Anna Kay. May you always exemplify God's grace.

Special thanks go to Nancy I. Sanders, who taught me how to write for children. And I thank God for allowing me to be His scribe.

The Girl's Guide to Manners (and all that good stuff)
©2014 by Tina M. Cho, second printing
ISBN 10: 1-58411-151-8
ISBN 13: 978-1-58411-151-1
RoseKidz reorder #: LP48221
JUVENILE NONFICTION / Religion / Christianity / Christian Life

RoseKidz
An imprint of Rose Publishing, Inc.
17909 Adria Maru Lane
Carson, CA 90746
www.Rose-Publishing.com

Cover illustrator: Laura Skibinsky
Interior illustrator: Shelley Dieterichs

Scriptures are from the Holy Bible: New International Version (North American edition), ©1973, 1978, 1984 by the International Bible Society. Used by permission of Zondervan Bible Publishers.

Printed in South Korea

Table of Contents

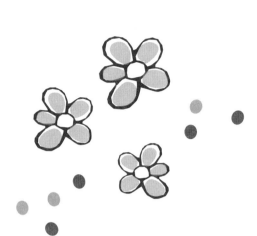

Hey Beautiful Girl!

I'm so glad you get to read this book! *The Girl's Guide to Manners (and all that good stuff)* is filled with stories, quizzes, puzzles, crafts, recipes, Bible verses, and activities to help you become a Christian girl full of good manners. You already know this, but—you're growing up! And the best person you can be is God's graceful girl inside and out. This book will show you what manners in action look like. You'll learn about etiquette and table manners, how to be poised, proper behavior and safety on social media, and how to host others in your home.

Perhaps you've heard of princesses going to charm school or training. Learning proper manners isn't just for nobility. God wants us all to look and act our best so that we can attract people to Jesus. The Bible is full of verses that show us how to live.

From history trivia to diary pages to questions and answers, you'll discover how you can be the ultimate girl of good manners. You might surprise your family with a whole new you! Let's begin!

Wishing you God's best!

Tina M. Cho

Chapter 1
A Heart Full of Grace

But you, O Lord, are a compassionate and gracious God, slow to anger, abounding in love and faithfulness. ~Psalm 86:15

Emma's Ink Pen

"I'm so glad we're in the same group for our field trip to the natural science museum," said Sophia to Emma while riding on the bus. "I'm glad Mom is our parent volunteer."

"Me too," said Emma, smiling. "I just love field trips. I wonder what we'll see."

"I'm just happy to be away from school," said Sophia.

The bus pulled into the museum parking lot. The students filed out one by one and lined up with their parent volunteers. Emma, Sophia, and two other girls were in group one. Inside the lobby Mr. Taylor, their teacher, gave each group a clipboard for a museum scavenger hunt.

"The team who completes their scavenger hunt first wins a prize from the museum," said Mr. Taylor. "Stay with your group at all times. We'll meet at noon for lunch."

"Okay, girls, where should we start?" asked Emma's mom.

"I want to see the animals," said Emma. After checking the map, they headed upstairs to the third floor.

"Keep your eyes open for the grizzly bear," said Emma. "I just read a question about it on our handout."

"Here are the forest animals," shouted Sophia. "The grizzly bear is probably down this hall." All the girls scurried behind Sophia.

"I found it!" yelled Sophia, jumping up and down. Emma dug in her pocket and pulled out a pretty pink pen with a sparkle heart dangling from the top.

"Let's see. How many pounds can a grizzly bear weigh?" she asked. The girls read the sign.

"A grizzly can weigh up to 800 pounds," read Sophia. "Yay, we have one question done."

Emma carefully took off the cap of her pink pen and wrote the answer. The scent of cotton candy wafted from her pen.

"Mmmm, something smells like cotton candy," said Sophia dreamily.

"It's my new pen," said Emma. "It's scented." Each girl took a whiff.

"Where did you find it?" asked Sophia.

"At the small gift store by my house," said Emma. She twisted the cap back on and hid it safely in her pocket.

"Why don't we take turns writing the answers?" asked Sophia.

"Okay," said Emma, handing her the clipboard.

"Can I carry your cotton candy pen?" asked Sophia. "I'm your best friend. You know I always take care of your stuff."

Emma hesitated. "Well, I guess. Just be careful not to lose it. Do you have a pocket?"

"My jacket has a pocket right here," said Sophia.

Emma took the pen out of her pocket and slowly handed it over to Sophia.

"Don't worry, Emma," said Sophia.

"Let's go look at the gems now," said Emma. "I love sparkly jewelry." The girls hurried downstairs to the rocks and minerals exhibit.

"Look at this," said Emma pointing to a shiny crystal.

"Our instructions say to write down the name of the gem sitting next to an emerald," said Sophia. The group pressed their noses against the display glass hunting for an emerald.

"Wouldn't it be fun to dress up in all this jewelry?" asked Emma. The girls nodded their heads.

"I can't find the emerald," said Emma. "It should be in this case with all the pretty rocks."

They checked one more time. "Not here," said Sophia. "Let's try this way."

"These are lava rocks and moon rocks," said Emma. "They're kind of ugly."

"I think I found it," said Sophia. The girls stared at the big emerald.

"What's that ugly rock next to it?" asked Emma.

Sophia read the sign. "You're not going to believe this, but it says it's a diamond. An uncut diamond, still in the rough."

Sophia dug in her pocket for Emma's pen. It wasn't there. She tried the other side.

"Why don't you write down the answer?" asked Emma.

"Umm, your pen seems to be gone," said Sophia with a panicked look on her face.

"What?" said Emma. "I thought you put it in your pocket."

"I did," said Sophia. "It must have fallen out."

"We can buy a new one," said Emma's mom.

"But it was the last cotton candy one," said Emma with a scowl.

"I'm really sorry," said Sophia.

Emma's emotions were topsy-turvy, but she remembered what her Sunday school teacher said about showing grace to others. "That's all right," she said. "It was just an accident."

Emma's mom gave the girls a pen to use.

"Come on," said Emma. "We have a scavenger hunt to win."

What Do YOU Think?

1. Why was Emma upset with Sophia?

_____

_____

_____

2. Do you have a favorite pen or item that you don't like to share? What is it?

_____

_____

_____

3. Can you think of a time when you should have shown grace to someone instead of lashing out at them?_____

_____

_____

_____

 QUIZ Grace in Action

Can you recognize a graceful situation? **Circle T for true or F for false.**

T or F 1. Grace is when you buy a bag of potato chips and eat them in front of all your friends.

T or F 2. Grace is when you hog a conversation so that no one else has room to talk.

T or F 3. Grace is when you invite friends over to your house, but they have to do your activities, even if they don't want to.

T or F 4. Grace is shown by the golden rule, which jewelry makers use when measuring and weighing gold.

T or F 5. Grace is when you forget your homework, and the teacher says you can bring it tomorrow with no grade deduction.

T or F   6. Grace is when the pizza delivery guy is late, and you still give him a generous tip.

T or F   7. Grace is when your little sister spills grape juice all over your white sweater, and you don't get mad.

T or F   8. Grace is when you forget to clean your room, and your mom still buys you a chocolate shake.

T or F   9. Grace is when you are late to softball practice, but the coach still lets you hit in the first inning.

T or F   10. Grace is when God sent Jesus, His only Son, to die for our sin.

Check your answers below:

1. **False**. A graceful girl is just the opposite. She would share her bag of chips with others.

2. **False**. A graceful girl would listen to others and allow them to talk.

3. **False**. A graceful girl puts others first. She would do activities her friends want to do.

4. **False**. A graceful girl knows that the golden rule is to do unto others as you would have them do to you.

5. **False**. You really deserve to have a lower grade since it was late. But because of your teacher's grace, you can smile. Be thankful for your teacher.

6. **True**. Because the pizza delivery guy was late, he doesn't deserve much of a tip. But to show grace, you give him a generous amount.

7. **True**. A graceful girl can control her emotions. Good job!

8. **True**. What a great mom you have! You could have been grounded.

9. **True**. Hug your coach. You could have run laps.

10. **True**. Jesus is perfect, without sin. Yet He chose to die for us and take our punishment on the cross. He loves us that much. Do you believe in His love for you?

How Did You Do?

❋ **If you got fewer than five questions right**, you will need to pay close attention to this book. Perhaps you could use more grace in your life. You may have been snubbing friends and family and weren't aware of it.

✳ **If you got 5-7 questions right**, you are doing great in recognizing grace. Be alert when you're with others so that you can extend grace to them.

✳ **If you got 8-10 questions right**, you go girl! Continue showing grace to people all around you and making them smile.

Fun Facts

A Diamond in the Rough

Diamonds are dug from deep inside the earth in mines around the world. Extreme heat helps create the diamond. To become a brilliant diamond, it must undergo many steps. The roughness must be removed. A planner studies the diamond to determine how to get the most value. Then it is cut. A diamond is the hardest substance known. Therefore, a diamond must be used to cut another diamond. The jewel is rounded into shape. A worker polishes the diamond to make it shine. You are like a rough diamond. God has a special plan and design for you, but first the rough edges must be removed. Learning about God's grace is one of the first steps into becoming a girl of brilliance. Shine for Jesus!

On Jan. 26, 1905, the largest rough diamond ever found was discovered in the Premier Diamond Mine in South Africa. At first, because of its large size, the manager thought it was an ugly crystal and threw it away! Thankfully, it was recovered. The diamond, weighing 3,106 carats, was named the Cullinan Diamond, after Thomas Cullinan, discoverer of the mine. The Transvaal government (which later became part of South Africa) purchased the diamond and gave it to King Edward VII of England in 1908 as a gift. The diamond was cut into nine gems by a gem cutter in Holland. This was no easy task, as the first blow broke the knife, and the diamond remained whole! The second blow split the diamond in half. Then for the next eight months grinding and polishing the diamond took place. The nine gems weighed 1,055.8 carats. The largest of them all, named the Cullinan I, is inlaid in the Sovereign's Scepter, and the Cullinan II is embedded in the Imperial State Crown, both of which are currently used by the Queen of England. The seven other gems were set into brooches and other jewelry for King Edward's wife, Queen Alexandra, and his daughter-in-law, Queen Mary. These brooches are now on display in the Tower of London.

 ## Make a Beaded Bracelet
(and remember to shine for Jesus!)

What You Need:

* Embroidery floss (3 colors)
* Scissors
* Beads
* Tape

What You Do:

1. Use only 2 strands from each color and tie one end of all the strands into a knot. Tape that knot onto a table.

2. Braid the strands, separating into the three colors. To braid, lay the strands on a table with the three colors divided into three sections. Grab the left color strands and cross over the middle strands. That middle strand now becomes the left strand. Then grab the right strand and cross over the new middle strand. Then back to the left strand, cross it over the middle. Then grab the right strand and cross the new middle strand. The pattern keeps repeating left, right, left, right until you're at the end.

3. Take a tiny piece of tape and wrap the ends really tight so that you can pull the braided floss through your beads.

4. Make a knot on your bracelet where you want the first bead to lie. Depending on the size of the hole, you might have to make a double knot. Slide the bead onto the floss all the way to the knot. Then make another knot on the other side of the bead to secure the bead into place. Repeat for your other beads.

5. When finished beading, tie the two ends of the bracelet together. Your bracelet is now ready to be worn.

For an easier bracelet, you can use jewelry string or a chenille wire and slide the beads on without braiding.

If you have extra floss and beads, make some bracelets for your friends to show grace to them. When you wear the bracelet, think about how you will shine and sparkle for Jesus!

Dear Anna,

At church I always hear adults say, "show grace to someone." And my grandma tells me I should be more graceful. What exactly is grace?

From: Confused

Dear Confused,

Grace has more than one meaning. Grace is being kind, courteous, and showing favor to people even when they don't deserve it. A person is also graceful if she moves with beauty and ease.

Dear Anna,

My older sister is so rude to me every day. This morning she locked the bathroom door and wouldn't let me in, and I was almost late for the bus. How can I show manners to her when I'm angry with her?

From: Little Sister

Dear Little Sister,

First, you need to forgive your sister, even if she doesn't apologize. The Bible says we are to be forgiving. Then you can show grace by doing something kind for her. Make her a gift or help her with one of her chores. Let her know you love her. Your love will eventually win her over. This is grace in action!

. . . .

Dear Anna,

I'm a quiet person and like to be alone. Do you think that's wrong? How can I show grace?

From: Quiet Mouse

Dear Quiet Mouse,

God's plan is for us to reach out to others. You can pray and ask God to help you talk to people. You will be happier if you have helped another friend. Jesus always reached out to people. After he spent time with the crowd, Jesus left to be alone and pray. Think about how you can reach out to others first before you spend time by yourself.

. . . .

God's View

God showed us the ultimate example of grace. Would you take the place of a guilty prisoner who was sentenced to die? Jesus did. He took your place! The Bible says the punishment for sin is death. But Jesus took your place when He died on the cross for your sins. If you believe and trust in Him as your Savior, you will go to heaven when you die. This grace shows God's great love and kindness for you. Whom can you share God's grace with today?

*But God demonstrates His own love for us in this: While we were still sinners, Christ died for us. ~ **Romans 5:8***

For it is by grace you have been saved, through faith—and this not from yourselves, it is the gift of God—not by works, so that no one can boast.

*~ **Ephesians 2:8-9***

*Bear with each other and forgive one another if any of you has a grievance against someone. Forgive as the Lord forgave you. ~**Colossians 3:1***

*Be kind and compassionate to one another, forgiving each other, just as in Christ God forgave you. ~**Ephesians 4:32***

 Trivia!

Many parents choose names that mean "grace" for their daughters. Some of these names are Carissa, Grace, Jenna, Karis, Anna or Ana, Nancy, Shawna, and Hannah.

If you have a name that means grace, wear it proudly. If you know someone whose name means "grace," share their name's meaning with them. What does your name mean? If you're not sure, you can look it up on the Internet on baby names web sites.

Does your name fit your personality?

My name means: _____

_____

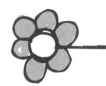

 Profile: A Woman of Grace

RAHAB *(Joshua 2:1-24, 6:22-25, Matthew 1:5)*

Rahab was a woman who lived in the city of Jericho, enemy territory of the Israelites. She lived in a unique house that was part of the city wall. She and her people melted with fear when they heard of how God dried up the

Red Sea for the Israelites to escape the Egyptians and the Israelites' defeat of two kings. So imagine how startled she was when two enemy Israelite spies showed up at her door!

The king of Jericho found out the spies were at her house, and he demanded she turn them in. Rahab told the king's messenger that she didn't know who the spies were and that at dusk they had left the city. She encouraged the king's messenger to look for them in the countryside.

Rahab showed grace to the Israelite spies. Instead of turning them in (usually one would turn in the enemy) she hid them among the flax on her roof. Flax is a plant that can grow almost four feet tall. If the stalks were bundled together and drying on her roof, the men could've easily hidden under them.

After the messenger left, Rahab went up to the roof and told the men what had happened. She acknowledged their God is the God of heaven and earth. Rahab requested kindness in return. She asked that the spies spare her family's lives when Israel came to attack Jericho.

The spies told Rahab that if she kept her promise not to turn them in, they would save her family. She let the spies escape out her window using a scarlet rope. The men told Rahab to bring her family to her house. When they returned to attack the city and saw the scarlet cord tied to the window, they would spare her family.

And that is exactly what happened. The spies returned grace to Rahab. Her father, mother, brothers, and all her relatives were rescued.

God blessed Rahab for showing grace. She married a man named Salmon, and they had a boy named Boaz. Boaz married a woman named Ruth, and they had a son named Obed. Obed was the grandfather of King David. And David was in the line in which Jesus would be born. So essentially, Rahab was an ancestral great-grandmother of Jesus Christ!

God will bless you when you show grace to others.

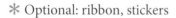 Make it! Scented Bath Crystals

These scented bath crystals will help you scrub away your roughness and polish yourself to shine for Jesus.

What You Need:

* Epsom salts
* Sandwich bags (the zip kind)
* Funnel
* Perfume or scented essential oils
* Paper towels or wax paper
* Small jars like baby food jars or sandwich bags (the non-zip kind) and pretty twisters
* Optional: ribbon, stickers

What You Do:

1. Use the funnel to pour Epsom salts into a sandwich bag that zips shut.
2. Add 1-2 sprays of your favorite perfume or a few drops of the essential oil into the bag.
3. Zip the bag.
4. Knead it with your fingers until all the salts are coated.
5. Dump the salt onto wax paper or paper towels. Let it dry for 10 minutes.
6. Put the bath salt into a baby food jar or baggie. Decorate with ribbon or stickers.

When you take a bath,
add 2 tablespoons of bath salt and enjoy!

 Letters to **GOD.**

 Dear God,

Today my class went on a field trip to the science museum. Sophia got to be in my mom's group with me. We were having fun on the museum scavenger hunt until Sophia lost my cotton candy pen. I didn't really want to share it, but she's my best friend. I wanted to yell at her. Instead I forgave her like I should do. That's what I learned in church.

Tonight Mom took me back to the gift store where we bought the pen. There was a new box of cotton candy scented pens! I bought one for Sophia and me. I can't wait to give it to her. She'll be so surprised. As we were driving home, Mom said, "I'm proud of you for how you handled the situation with Sophia. That was a true example of grace."

"Thanks, Mom," I said. "I'm glad I didn't explode with anger. I didn't want to ruin my friendship with my best friend."

I guess I learned to think before I react so that I can show Jesus' love and grace to my friends. I wrapped the pen in pretty paper and will give it to Sophia first thing in the morning. My insides are tingling with happiness.

Good night!
Emma

Jot it Down!

Now it's your turn to journal about what you've learned about grace. Write how you've shown grace to others or how you've received grace from someone.

_____

_____

_____

_____

_____

_____

_____

_____

_____

_____

_____

_____

_____

_____

_____

_____

_____

Memory Verse Write the memory verse from the beginning of the chapter below. **(Psalm 86:15)** Memorize it and recite it to someone in your family. How can you share God's grace?

_____

_____

_____

A Heart Full of Kindness

Jesus' grace is loving kindness that He showed to you by dying on the cross. Believe in Him. Share His grace with your family and friends.

Prayer Dear God, thank You for Your grace. Help me to show Your loving kindness to others. In Jesus' name, Amen.

Chapter 2
A Heart Full of Respect

Do to others as you would have them do to you. ~Luke 6:31

Swimming with Misty

"Mom, Angelina is coming over to swim," said Misty.

"Next time it would be nice if you'd check with me first," said Mom. "Your brother's soccer game is at 5:00 P.M. You can't be late. It's 2:00 P.M. now."

"Why do I have to attend all his games?" asked Misty.

"We are family, and we are there for each other. Isaac came to all your dance recitals."

"Fine," Misty said and stormed off to the pool.

"And keep the noise down. You know Grandma is taking a nap," said Mom.

Misty dove off the diving board into the clear blue water. She loved swimming away her troubles and being by herself. Her thoughts were interrupted when Mom said Angelina had arrived.

"Why don't you come greet your guest?" asked Mom.

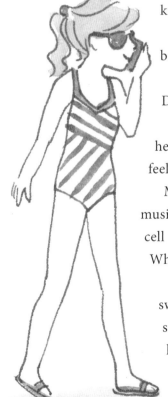

"Just tell her to come out to the pool. She knows the way," said Misty.

"Hi Misty," said Angelina with her swimming bag and with a towel wrapped around her waist.

"Hi," said Misty. "Eww, what's that smell? Did you eat burritos for lunch?"

"Yes, I did," said Angelina. She unwrapped her towel and stepped into the pool. "The water feels good."

Misty got out of the pool and cranked up the music. She lay on the lawn chair and grabbed her cell phone. She called another friend. "Hi Amy. What are you doing?"

Angelina decided to get some exercise swimming since Misty was obviously busy. She swam laps around the pool. As soon as Misty hung up, Angelina got out and sat in the chair beside her.

"This weekend my family is going on a

bike trail by the beach," said Angelina. "I'm so excited."

Ring, ring! "Hello," answered Misty, interrupting Angelina. She walked into the house, talking like it would be a long phone call.

Angelina jumped back into the pool. Soon Grandma walked out and sat in a chair.

"Oh, hi," said Angelina getting out. "I didn't know you were here." She turned off the music.

"That's ok," she said. "Misty doesn't seem to care."

"Would you like an ice cream cone?" asked Grandma.

"No thanks, I'm allergic to milk," said Angelina.

"Then how about some watermelon?" asked Grandma again.

"No thank you, I'm fine," said Angelina.

As Angelina and Grandma visited, Misty finally returned eating an ice cream cone. "Who turned off the music?" she said angrily. She turned the music on, threw her ice cream wrapper on the ground, and jumped into the pool. A big splash of water landed on Angelina's and Grandma's legs.

Mom walked out. "Misty, don't forget Isaac's soccer game at 5:00," she yelled. Misty ignored her and did a somersault in the water. "Misty, Misty!" yelled Mom.

"Do I really have to go?" she asked. Mom shook her head yes.

Misty got out of the pool and grabbed her cell phone again to play games. "How long has your grandma lived with you?" asked Angelina.

"For a couple of months," Misty replied, totally engrossed in her game.

Misty went into the kitchen and brought out a glass of water. Angelina and Grandma watched her sip the water and play. Finally Grandma spoke. "Angelina, would you like some water?"

"Yes, please," she said. Grandma hobbled into the house and brought out two ice waters.

Misty went back inside and brought out a plate of chocolate cupcakes. "Mom and I made these yesterday. Eat one."

"Do they have milk in them?" asked Angelina.

"I don't think so. Why?" asked Misty.

"Remember, I'm allergic to milk," said Angelina.

"Oh, don't be so picky, Angelina. You're not going to die if you eat a small cupcake," said Misty, picking one off the plate and shoving it into her hand. "Just taste it!" she demanded.

"Misty," said Grandma, "you don't force someone to eat something." Misty just ignored her and stared at her friend.

Angelina didn't want to upset her friend further, and so she took a generous bite of cupcake. "It's delicious," she said.

"Of course," said Misty. "I made them." She looked at the clock. 4:30 P.M. She jumped back into the pool.

Minutes later, Angelina yelled. "Misty, I'm breaking out with hives. I itch all over."

"Those cupcakes must have had some milk in them," said Grandma. Angelina used Misty's phone to call her mom.

"I have to go to the doctor," said Angelina.

"I'll go with you," said Misty. Both girls quickly changed their clothes.

Angelina's mom picked up the girls. The doctor gave Angelina some medicine.

"I'm sorry for making you eat the cupcake," said Misty. "I guess I wasn't much of a host today."

"That's okay," said Angelina. "My mom has a recipe for milk-free cupcakes. Why don't you come over tomorrow, and we can make them."

"Sure," said Misty. "I'd like that."

What Do YOU Think?

1. Can you name all the ways Misty showed disrespect?

_____

_____

_____

2. Do you know someone with food allergies? Who?

_____

_____

3. Is there a time you didn't show respect to someone? How could you have acted differently?

_____

_____

_____

PUZZLE Word Scramble

Unscramble the words below to see what respect and disrespect look like. Copy the bold letters onto the verse below.

Ways We Respect Others

1. **r**onoh _____

2. **e**ulva _____

3. **s**aeipr _____

4. ta**p**aeciper _____

5. re**m**adi _____

Ways We Disrespect Others

6. ahect _____

7. truh _____

8. lulby _____

9. gonire _____

10. fishesl _____

See the answers on page 192.

Show proper _____ _____ _____ _____ _____ _____ _____ to everyone:

Love the family of believers, fear God, honor the emperor. *~ 1 Peter 2:17*

Fun Facts

Respect in South Korea

Children in South Korea show respect to adults in many ways. When an older person comes to their home, they must stand, bow, and say hello. When the adult leaves, they stand, bow, and say good-bye. There are also different polite ways of speaking to adults. You wouldn't speak to your grandmother the same way you speak to your best friend. Korean children have to use special word endings on their verbs when addressing older people.

Just as respect is shown to the elderly, even more so, respect and honor should be shown to Jesus. The Bible says that one day every knee will bow and everyone will show respect to Jesus Christ.

Try It! Korean Bow

Practice a Korean bow to greet your parent when they come home. First, stand in front of a mirror. Move your head down and bend forward just slightly at the waist. That's it! To say hello in Korean, pronounce this quickly: *AN-Nyung-Ha-Sayo.*

Try showing respect to your parent or grandparent Korean style by bowing and saying hello.

Dear Anna,

My friend got in trouble at school for not showing respect to the teacher. Our teachers are always telling us to show respect. What is respect?

From: A Fourth Grader

Dear Fourth Grader,

Respect is thinking of others around you and putting their needs first. Respect is treating others as very special people. If everyone at school treated each other with respect, there would be fewer problems. In our society, older people are to be shown more respect. They're older, wiser, and have earned honor from others. For example, if you and an older person approach a door at the same time, step aside, and let the older person go first.

Dear Anna,

A new girl came to our school from Ghana, West Africa. She speaks differently and sometimes dresses in native clothing. Our teacher said we have to respect her culture. I've heard some kids making fun of her at recess. How can I show her respect?

From: A Concerned Friend

Dear Concerned Friend,

I am glad you want to help this new classmate. It must be awkward being in a new country. You can respect her culture by learning about it and telling others not to make fun of her. Perhaps your teacher will let the girl share about her country. Then everyone will feel more comfortable. The best thing you can do is to be her friend.

Dear Anna,

I have a friend who doesn't show respect to me. In fact, she's sort of a bully, always telling me what to do. She gets mad if I don't do what she says. In gym class, she calls me "slowpoke" in front of the others, which is so embarrassing. I don't want to be a tattle tale, but sometimes I don't even want to go to school. I want to avoid her. What should I do?

From: Jill

Dear Jill,

You should not have to put up with this kind of behavior. First, I would pray to God and tell Him about it. Then I'd ask the girl why she's acting this way. The world would tell you to get revenge or to get her back. But the Bible says to treat others as you want to be treated. The Bible says in 1 Thessalonians 5:15 not to pay back wrong for wrong. Instead we are to love our enemies. How can you show her extra kindness? This will change her heart. If she won't listen, then I'd seek adult help, like your parents and teacher. Bullying is wrong, and no one should have to put up with it.

. . . .

Dear Anna,

My older sister always comes in my room without knocking and borrows my stuff without asking. I tell her not to, but she won't listen to me. What should I do?

From: Frustrated Sister

Dear Frustrated Sister,

Respecting people's property is very important, and your bedroom and your things are your property to take care of. You could try making a sign that says "Please Knock" and hang it on the outside of your door, which means you should keep your door closed. If that doesn't work, try talking to your sister in a kind way and tell her your feelings. Maybe she doesn't realize it makes you angry. And if that doesn't do it, talk with your parents and see how they can help.

. . . .

God's View

God created all people and told us to love each other like we love ourselves. Jesus taught His disciples to serve others. He even told them the Son of Man came to serve, not to be served (Matthew 20:28). Our culture today says "It's all about ME!" But it's not about you. It's all about God's purpose for you. How can you reach out to others so that they will want to know God? There's an acronym for the word JOY. Jesus, Others, You. You should put Jesus first, Others second, and Yourself last. If you put this into practice, you'll have joy in Jesus. Do you treat others with respect so they can see God in you?

Do nothing out of selfish ambition or vain conceit. Rather, in humility value others above yourselves. ~ **Philippians 2:3**

Love the Lord your God with all your heart and with all your soul and with all your strength and with all your mind, and, love your neighbor as yourself .

~ *Luke 10:27*

Love is patient, love is kind. It does not envy, it does not boast, it is not proud. It does not dishonor others, it is not self-seeking, it is not easily angered, it keeps no record of wrongs. Love does not delight in evil but rejoices with the truth. It always protects, always trusts, always hopes, always perseveres. ~ *1 Corinthians 13:4-7*

Trivia!

When George Washington was sixteen years old, as part of a school assignment, he copied *Rules of Civility & Decent Behaviour In Company and Conversation*. There were 110 rules of behavior that dealt with how to be respectful of others. These rules were composed by French Jesuits in 1595. The first rule on the list is "Every Action done in Company, ought to be with Some Sign of Respect, to those that are Present." The 29th rule says, "When you meet with one of Greater Quality than yourself, Stop, and retire especially if it be at a Door or any Straight place to give way for him to Pass." George Washington lived up to these rules and became a man who earned respect.

Checklist for Being Respectful at Home

Life at home will be happy and smooth if everyone shows respect to each other. Look at this list. Check off ones you already do.

☐ I respect my siblings' privacy by not taking their things without asking or walking into their rooms without knocking.

☐ I keep my toys and stuff in my room rather than all over the house.

☐ I pick up my clothes so my mom doesn't have to do it.

☐ I throw dirty clothes in the hamper or laundry basket.

☐ I do my chores on time.

☐ I offer to help in the kitchen, cooking or setting the table.

☐ I share video games with my siblings, and let them choose games they want to play.

☐ I don't spend too much time on my cell phone, and when my parents ask me to turn it off, I do it right away.

☐ I take care of my body by keeping it clean—showering, making my hair nice, brushing my teeth, and keeping my clothes neat.

☐ When my parents are gone, I'm responsible and trustworthy, keeping our home in order.

☐ I spend time with my siblings playing a game or just spending quality time together instead of fighting.

☐ I'm respectful at the table, chewing with my mouth closed, and not slurping.

☐ At home, I'm careful not to make loud noises or stomping on the floor.

☐ I try to make my parents' life easier by helping out as much as I can.

☐ I don't read mail or e-mail unless it's addressed to me.

☐ I answer the phone politely and take messages if someone is gone.

☐ I don't yell at my family or mouth off to my parents.

☐ I introduce my friends who come over to my parents and siblings.

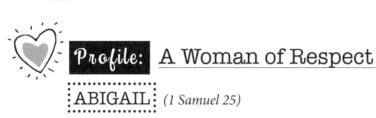

Profile: A Woman of Respect

ABIGAIL *(1 Samuel 25)*

David and his men hid from King Saul and camped out in the desert. King Saul wanted to kill David because he was more popular and a great warrior. David's campout was near Nabal's property. Nabal was a rich man who owned 1,000 goats and 3,000 sheep. He had a beautiful, intelligent wife named Abigail.

It was sheep-shearing season. Can you imagine giving 3,000 sheep a haircut? While Nabal's shepherds spread out to do the huge task, David's men basically protected Nabal's property and didn't disturb the shepherds even though David's men were hungry and lacked property of their own.

David decided to send ten of his men down to Nabal to ask for provisions (food) in his name. Since David's group had provided protection and didn't steal anything, shouldn't rich Nabal share some food during this festive time of sheep shearing?

The Bible states that Nabal was a mean man. He told David's men he didn't know who this David even was. And why should he share his bread, water, and meat with someone he didn't even know? Well, you can imagine David's reaction. David rounded up 400 of his men with their swords to go down and kill Nabal and his group.

Meanwhile, one of Nabal's servants had overheard the conversation between Nabal and David's men and told Abigail. The servant praised David, stating how wonderful his men had been to the shepherds. Immediately, Abigail prepared a bunch of food: 200 loaves of bread, 2 skins of wine, 5 prepared sheep, 200 cakes of pressed figs, about 37 liters of roasted grain, and 100 raisin cakes. All of this was loaded onto donkeys, with the servants and Abigail following.

The donkey caravan caught up with David's men in a ravine, while David was on his way to kill Nabal. Abigail showed respect to David by getting off her donkey and bowing her head to the ground right at David's feet. She apologized for what had happened and asked David to listen to her. In her carefully-worded speech, she told David God had kept him from getting revenge. She wanted David to accept her gift of food and said she believed David would become the next king.

David granted her request, accepted the food, and didn't kill Nabal. Instead he left the matter in God's hands. When Abigail returned home, Nabal was very drunk, and so she waited until morning to tell him about David. And when she did, Nabal's heart failed him. Ten days later the Lord struck him, and he died.

God blessed Abigail. When David heard Nabal had died, he asked Abigail to become his wife. Because she had shown respect, she had won David's heart.

Make it! Angelina's No-Milk Cupcakes

Let's bake! These no-milk cupcakes are a delicious snack to serve to your friends.

What You Need:

* 1 cup of sugar
* 1 tablespoon vinegar
* 1 teaspoon vanilla
* ⅓ cup of vegetable oil
* 1 cup of cold water
* 1 ½ cup of flour
* ¼ cup of cocoa powder
* 1 teaspoon baking soda
* ½ teaspoon salt
* 1 teaspoon cinnamon
* Optional: sprinkles
* 2 mixing bowls, spatula, cupcake pan, cupcake liners

What You Do:

1. Have a parent turn the oven to 350 degrees F (175 degrees C).
2. In a bowl, mix the sugar, vinegar, vanilla, oil and water.
3. In a separate bowl, mix the flour, cocoa powder, baking soda, salt, and cinnamon.
4. Gradually add the dry flour mixture into the wet sugar mixture. Stir.
5. Put cupcake liners into the pan. Fill each liner half full of batter. You can pour sprinkles on top.
6. Bake for 30-35 minutes. This makes 9 large cupcakes.

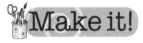 # Make it! Make an Appreciation Card and Deliver a Cupcake

You can put respect into action by making cards for people you respect and delivering them one of the cupcakes you baked and decorated. They'll be pleasantly surprised!

What You Need:

* Cardstock
* Sponge
* Paint
* Scissors
* Paper plate
* Markers
* Pen
* Optional: glitter, sequins

What You Do:

1. First, make a stencil. Decide on an image for the front of your appreciation card. It could be a cupcake, something that can be drawn in one piece. Draw the image on one sheet of cardstock.

2. You're going to cut the image out without cutting the sides of the paper. To do that, slightly fold the paper in the middle of your image and make a snip with your scissors. Insert your scissors into the hole, and cut out your image. Discard the image. What's left in the paper should be the outline of your image or your stencil.

3. To make the card, fold a piece of cardstock in half. Position the stencil on the front of the card where you want the image to be stamped.

4. Pour a little paint onto a paper plate. Dip the sponge into the paint and then wipe off the excess on the plate. Stamp the sponge onto the stencil so that the whole area is covered with paint. Be sure to tightly hold the stencil in place.

5. When finished stamping, lift the stencil up. Your image is revealed on the front of the cover.

6. You can decorate your image using markers, glitter, and sequins. Write appreciative words on the card such as, "You're sweet as a cupcake. I appreciate you. You're the sweetest friend. Thanks for all you do."

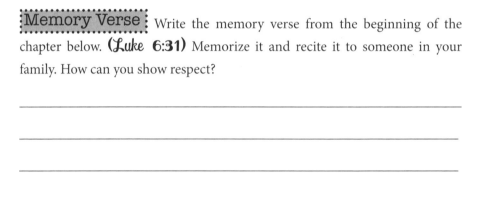

Deliver a card and cupcake to people whom you want to show respect.

Memory Verse Write the memory verse from the beginning of the chapter below. **(Luke 6:31)** Memorize it and recite it to someone in your family. How can you show respect?

_____

_____

_____

_____

<u>A Heart Full of Kindness</u> A Christian girl of manners also treats others with respect. See how many people you can make smile today. Put yourself last and serve other people's needs first. Remember the Golden Rule!

 Prayer **Dear God,** help me to treat others how I would want to be treated. I hope I can serve others like You did. In Jesus' name, Amen.

 Letters to **GOD.**

Dear God,

I acted like a total flop yesterday. I was disrespectful to everyone, and I made my good friend have an allergic reaction. Angelina's medicine did the trick, and her hives disappeared. Her mom dropped me off at my brother's soccer game just in time for me to see Isaac kick a goal. I told Isaac I'd be on time to his next game and cheer extra loud. I had lots of people to apologize to.

I told Mom I was sorry for inviting a friend without her permission and said I would try to stop complaining. I watched a movie with Grandma and made her hot tea. I do appreciate having her around. I just never showed it.

Today I went to Angelina's house and enjoyed a delicious Mexican meal. Afterward, we baked the no-milk cupcakes. I can't even tell they're different. The coolest part was decorating the cupcakes with sprinkles and colored sugar.

Angelina said, "Let's pass these out to our friends tomorrow."

I agreed. "We can give each person a compliment and a cupcake to show them we appreciate them."

I can't wait for tomorrow.

Good night!
Misty

Jot it Down!

Now it's your turn to write about what you've learned about respect. You can write how you've shown respect to others.

_____

_____

_____

_____

_____

_____

_____

_____

_____

_____

_____

_____

_____

_ _

_____

_____

_____

Chapter 3
Cyber Safe & Savvy

Therefore encourage one another and build each other up, just as in fact you are doing. ~1 Thessalonians 5:11

Jordyn's Post Goes Viral

After school, Jordyn dug her phone out of her backpack to check her recent messages.

R U coming over 4 supper? TTYL. From Isabella

Bring your book. I rlly want 2 read it. Don't' be L8. Thx. From Isabella

Yes, c u at 6 with book. g2g. From Jordyn

While Jordyn waited for her brother Seth, she flipped through some pictures on her cell phone. Last Saturday night Isabella had a sleepover at her house. And during a truth or dare game, Isabella had to stick a whole slice of pizza in her mouth. *This is such a great picture,* thought Jordyn. She opened her face page account and uploaded the photo of Isabella. She typed, "My BFF has a big mouth. Haha." Satisfied with the post, she met her brother coming down the sidewalk.

Once home, she turned on her computer to check her e-mail. Then Jordyn opened her face page account. A big photo of Isabella stuffing the pizza in her mouth was plastered on the screen. So far it had 20 likes. "Oh no, three other friends shared the picture. Isabella is going to be mad at me!"

Jordyn grabbed her phone out of her backpack to check messages.

What's going on? People r texting if I like pizza. IDK. From Isabella

Someone sent "Big-mouth Izzy" From Isabella

Did u show my pic? From Isabella

Forget about supper. I don't want to c u. From Isabella

Jordyn quickly typed: *I'm sorry. Plz 4give me. I did share your pic only cuz I thought it was funny.*

I didn't mean to hurt u. From Jordyn

R U there? From Jordyn

Jordyn called Isabella on

the phone. No answer. "Pick up, Izzy. I'm sorry." Still no answer.

What am I going to do? Isabella is my best friend. Jordyn went into the kitchen.

"Mom, I'm staying home for supper."

"I thought you were going to Isabella's."

"Well, she's mad at me, and so I'll be eating here."

Jordyn went into her bedroom and got out her homework. *Ring, ring.* Someone wanted to video chat. She accepted on her computer. It was her school friend Shay.

"Hi, Jordyn. You don't look too happy."

"Have you heard what happened?" asked Jordyn.

"Yeah. That's why I called. People in our class are texting like crazy about the picture you posted," said Shay.

"And I was only trying to be funny," said Jordyn. "I didn't know it would turn out like this. I guess I learned my lesson about posting photos."

"So what's your plan to undo it?" asked Shay.

"I haven't come up with anything yet. But I will."

"Let me know if I can help you," said Shay. "I have to go now. Bye."

"Thanks, Shay. Bye."

Jordyn stared at the picture of her and Isabella when they were in kindergarten together. It hung above her desk. "That's it," she said. "I know how to fix this problem."

She pulled out her old photo album and found pictures of her and Isabella growing up together. With her cell phone, she took a snapshot of each picture. Then she uploaded them into her computer.

Her mother had shown her a picture sharing web site and had created an account. Jordyn signed in and uploaded the pictures. Then she typed a description of each picture. A new feature allowed her to add special borders and dialog tags. Then she wrote a poem for the cover of the album.

Isabella

You're my best friend forever since kindergarten.

We're sisters from the heart that can't be apart.

Finished! Jordyn went to the kitchen and quickly ate.

"Mom, I need to ride my bike over to see Isabella."

"That's fine, dear," said Mom. "Be home before dark."

Jordyn stuck her phone in a purse and rode to Isabella's house.

After Jordyn rang the bell, Isabella's mother answered.

"Can I see Isabella?"

"Why, sure, Jordyn. She's in her room."

Jordyn knocked on Isabella's door and walked in. Isabella was reading a book.

"Hi, Izzy. I just had to see you. I'm really sorry about what happened. You know I would never do anything to hurt you. I just thought that picture was really funny. I took the photo off my face page."

"I know you wouldn't be cruel," said Isabella. "It's just that I received so many mean messages. I can't believe how people jump on the chance to make fun of someone."

"I made something for you," said Jordyn, and she took out her phone and showed her the online photo album of their friendship.

Isabella gave her a hug. "Hugging a real person is better than a cyber hug," laughed Jordyn.

What Do YOU Think?

1. What was Jordyn's problem?

_____

_____

_____

_____

2. Write a rule or reminder Jordyn should have thought about before posting the picture.

_____

_____

_____

_____

3. Have you ever sent something over the Internet or a text message that you wished you could get back?

_____

_____

_____

_____

A Digital Look at Yourself

Before you polish yourself into a beautiful Christian girl on the inside and out, let's stop and take a photo. Ask someone to take a picture of you. Stand with good posture. Be proud of the person God made you to be. You can use this photo later to share with your friends and family online. If you have a digital camera or camera phone, computer, and printer, you can print the picture. Glue it into the frame on this page. Color the frame.

Fun Facts

Did You Know?

Before there were camera phones and digital cameras, your parents and grandparents probably used a camera with film. They inserted the film into the camera, and each time a picture was taken, it left an image on the film. When the film was used up, it was taken to a store to be developed.

With technology constantly changing and people wanting photographs as soon as possible, digital cameras were installed on cell phones. Now it's convenient to take a picture anytime and view it immediately. And even more amazing, the picture just taken can be shared immediately!

Guidelines for Photos

Sharing photos is fun, and if you follow these guidelines, your friends and family will be pleased with your photography skills.

- Only take appropriate photos of yourself and others. Never take pictures of naked people. Remember, you want to attract people to Jesus Christ through your behavior.
- Never post a photo to be mean or to hurt someone's feelings.
- Before you post a photo of others to a photo sharing site, always ask the person's permission. Before you post any picture, ask your parents if it's okay. Sometimes when posting a photo, it reveals your location details. You always want to be cautious for reasons of safety.

Dear Anna,

Some mean girls at my school sent made-up rumors about my friend and texted them to our classmates.

From: Hurting Heart

Dear Hurting Heart,

First, I would talk to your friend and tell her how much you care for her. Tell her these other classmates might be jealous about something and that's why they made up these rumors. Jesus says to pray for your enemies and fight evil with good. So after praying about the situation and for those who hurt your friend, try to ignore what happened and be nice to the others. If it continues, find out who is involved and talk to them about how it's not nice to make up lies and gossip about others. Ask them to send a new text apologizing. If they continue the behavior, get a teacher and parents involved.

Dear Anna,

I made some new friends, but they often text each other when we are together, and they start giggling. But they don't send me the texts, and I begin to think they are texting mean things about me and joking about me. What should I do?

From: Texting Friend

Dear Texting Friend,

The best thing is to be honest and truthful. Ask your friends what they are giggling about. Tell them you didn't receive the same text. If they are laughing about you, then they aren't the right friends to have. A true friend loves at all times. And love doesn't hurt others and make them feel insecure.

Dear Anna,

Some boys at my school send inappropriate texts. Some of my friends get them. I'm worried some might be sent to me on my cell phone.

From: Worried

Dear Worried,

Don't hang out with others who don't know the appropriate way to act. Never give out your personal information to those who shouldn't have it. And if you receive an inappropriate text, show it to your parents. You can always change to a different account if this continues.

Dear Anna,

My close friend met a boy online and talks about him constantly. But she has never seen him in person. Now she says he is planning to meet her at the bus station when he comes to visit her. It doesn't seem right to me. How can I get through to her?

From: Concerned Friend

Dear Concerned Friend,

First, tell your friend that meeting people online could be dangerous because people aren't always who they say they are. An older man could be posing as a younger boy and using a fake photo. Ask her to cancel the meeting, or if she really wants to meet him, to bring a parent. Share with her that she has plenty of time for boyfriends later in life. Right now, tell her you want to do things with her, without boys!

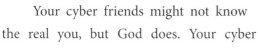

God's View

God knew you before you were born. He knows everything about you from how many hairs you have on your head to every tear that you cry. He knows your every thought and every problem. He knows your friends and whom you talk to. He sees everything you do, everything you look at online.

Your cyber friends might not know the real you, but God does. Your cyber identity might be different from the real you, but God wants others to know who you are so that they can come to love Him. How much time do you spend on technology? Instead, spend time with loved ones next to you. Live in the real world that God created for us to enjoy. Online relationships and activities can't duplicate the awesome experiences that you can enjoy face to face.

The eyes of the Lord are on the righteous, and His ears are attentive to their cry. ~ **Psalm 34:153**

Indeed, the very hairs of your head are all numbered. Don't be afraid; you are worth more than many sparrows. ~ **Luke 12:7**

Do not be misled: "Bad company corrupts good character."
~ **1 Corinthians 15:33**

And let us consider how we may spur one another on toward love and good deeds, not giving up meeting together, as some are in the habit of doing, but encouraging one another—and all the more as you see the Day approaching. ~ *Hebrews 10:24-25*

Fun Facts

Phone Etiquette

- Use your cell phone respectfully.
- Speak clearly and make sure you let the other person speak.
- Be a good listener. A good listener is well-liked and gains friends.
- If you're in a public area, talk with a soft voice or go somewhere private to speak.
- Turn off your ringer at church and other public places.

Video Game Etiquette

- If you're with other people, don't use your phone for gaming. Instead, talk to your friends and family.
- When company arrives, turn off your games, greet and visit with them.
- When it's time to eat, stop playing games.
- Never whine or complain when your parents ask you to stop playing. Gaming is a privilege.

Profile: A Woman of Truth

ESTHER *(Esther 2-7)*

King Xerxes, a Persian king whose empire stretched from India to Ethiopia, found himself without a queen. He had dismissed the former Queen Vashti because she had disobeyed him. So the king's attendants suggested he find a new queen by having beautiful young women brought to Hegai, who would train the women for the position.

One of these candidates for queen was Esther, a Jewess who had been taken captive from Israel by the king of Babylon. Esther was an orphan, raised by her cousin Mordecai, who treated her as his own daughter. Esther was beautiful and won Hegai's favor. For twelve months Esther received beauty treatments and special food. Perhaps she learned how to act in a royal court. She probably carried herself with poise and confidence. Indeed, God was with her, and the king chose her to be the next queen.

Esther excelled in her position; however, she kept a secret from everyone—the fact that she was a Jew. One day the king promoted one of his nobles named Haman, and all the other royal officials bowed to him. But Esther's cousin Mordecai refused to bow. When Haman found out Mordecai was a Jew, he devised an evil plan to destroy all the Jewish people. Mordecai dressed in mourning clothes and wept by the king's gate. Esther saw him so depressed, and she sent a messenger to him. Mordecai explained the situation about wicked Haman's plan and asked Esther to go to the king and plead for the Jewish people.

However, the kingdom had a law that no one was to see the king unless the king had sent for them. Otherwise, the punishment was death. But if the king held out his golden scepter, that person's life would be spared.

So Esther made a plan. She sent a message to Mordecai for him and all the Jews to fast for three days. After three days, she would see the king, even if it meant death.

On the third day, Esther dressed in a royal gown and entered the king's hall bravely with poise and confidence. When the king saw her, he held out his golden scepter and asked her request.

Instead of telling the king the horrible situation, Esther invited the king and Haman to a banquet on the following day. At the banquet, Esther told the king the truth of the evil plan to kill her people. When the king asked who was responsible, Esther pointed at Haman. He was hung on the gallows he'd made for Mordecai.

Queen Esther would've never saved her people if it wasn't for her courage to communicate clearly and speak the truth during a difficult time. By doing so, her message was heard and accepted by the king. The truth cuts through all the lies; a person who lives and speaks the truth is respected.

Let's Practice Cyber Manners

E-mails

It's fun to get e-mail. But before you reply, think about what you want to say, and reread what you typed. Once you hit the send button, you can't get it back. Only e-mail appropriate messages and photos, no bad words. You never know who will see your messages. If someone confides in you, don't forward their messages to others. Never write an e-mail when you're angry. You can't retract your words. Also, don't type in all capital letters. That's the same as shouting. Remember, deleted items are still traceable. Never reply to spam e-mails, as these are strangers looking to get your information.

Texting

Receiving immediate messages is awesome. But just like with e-mail, use it wisely. Be sensitive to those around you and refrain from texting at mealtimes, in line at a store, or when you're with other people. They want to chat with you, not watch you chat with others on your phone. Sometimes messages can be misunderstood. Use emoticons to accompany some of your texts.

Face page messages

These sites are great to connect with lots of friends and family at once. But obey the rules these sites have and follow your parent's directions for safety. Some sites have an age requirement. Think before you post a message or photo. Ask yourself, would you want your mom to see this? If not, it shouldn't be shared. People can share your posts, and it can spread like wildfire.

Don't make fun of others on social media. Remember to do to others as you want them to do to you. Before posting photos of others, get their permission. Never accept friend requests from strangers. If someone posts a photo or comment about you that you don't like, you can kindly ask them to remove it. If anyone makes you feel uncomfortable, threatens, or pressures you into doing something  that isn't right, unfriend and block them and tell a parent. If you use these sites wisely, they can be a great tool to connect with others.

Photo sharing

Photo sharing is a great way to share your happiness with others. But do it carefully. Only share appropriate photos with people you know. If someone else is in the photo, get their permission before sharing it. If someone else took the picture, and you don't have the copyright (it doesn't belong to you), don't share it.

Information sharing

Many websites ask you for private information because they want to sell you things or collect data about you. Never give out your personal information without your parent's permission. Never give out your address and phone number online. Only visit websites that are safe.

Video chat

This is a great tool to connect with long distance relatives and friends. Speak clearly so they can understand you. Look presentable in front of the camera. Sit with good posture, smile, and keep the conversation flowing. Only video chat and message with people you know. Never accept invitations from strangers.

 **Blogging**

Some kids do have blogs where they share information, maybe book reviews or class projects. You can start a free blog with your parent's permission on a topic that you feel like an expert.

Be careful with the information and photos you share on your blogs. Make sure it's all original content written by you. People will sue if you've copied their words or photos. Manage your comments that people can leave you. You want to approve appropriate comments. Spammers can leave hateful messages that you wouldn't want your blog to publish.

Digital Fun

Using the frame, print a digital picture that you sent or was sent to you and paste it in—a picture that really made you laugh or makes you happy each time you see it. That's what photo sharing is all about!

Help Someone Connect

Sometimes older people don't know how to use new technology, but it can often open up a whole new world to them. Show your grandmother or grandfather how to search for information online, maybe search for their hobbies (or trivia about their favorite TV show or movie star).

Help them open an e-mail account. Help them connect with their children, grandkids or friends who live far away. Show them how to use a photo sharing site: post pictures of them and see who responds. One grandmother gained thousands of fans when her grandson posted a picture of her sticking out her tongue, which was colored blue from a piece of candy she was eating. She became an online sensation!

Make it! Online Photo Album

Many photo sharing sites allow you to make an online photo album which you can share with friends.

1. With your parent's help, select an online photo site.
2. Download your photos from your phone or digital camera onto your computer.
3. Upload your photos from your computer onto the photo site, following their instructions.
4. Most sites let you arrange the pictures in the order that you want and

type captions.

5. Check to see if you can add borders to the pictures or any other fun stuff.

6. Preview your album, and share it with family and friends if that option is available.

7. If you want hard copies of your photos, ask your parents to help you place an order.

Memory Verse Write the memory verse from the beginning of the chapter below. **(1 Thessalonians 5:11)** Memorize it and recite it to someone in your family. What does this verse say about connecting with others?

_____

_____

_____

 <u>**A Heart Full of Kindness**</u> A Christian girl of manners makes connections with people to share God with them. She is a model in behavior and speech.

Prayer **Dear God,** Thank you for all the ways I can connect with family and friends. Help me to be respectful and kind in every way. In Jesus' name, Amen.

 Letters to **GOD.**

 ## Dear God,

Isabella loved my online photo album and the poem I wrote. She gave me permission to post it on my face page. So I did. It's gotten 30 likes and 4 shares. Classmates are texting how cute we were in the lower grades. The funny thing is that now other kids at school are sharing online photo albums of them and their friends. Thankfully, everyone is leaving positive comments.

Our teacher found out about our photo sharing. She liked it and asked Isabella and me to help her with the class blog. She said she would love for us to upload pictures of the class and write captions. I guess our parents like snooping at what we do all day in class.

My phone is overloaded with text messages. I don't think I'll ever get to bed on time. The last message was from a boy in class: "I want to try your pizza dare." I think I started something.

Good night!
Jordyn

Jot it Down!

Write what you learned about cyber manners, or what you learned about a cyber problem you were experiencing.

_____

_____

_____

_____

_____

_____

_____

_____

_____

_____

_____

_____

_____

_____

_____

_____

_____

Chapter 4
Dress for Godliness

Your beauty should not come from outward adornment, such as elaborate hairstyles and the wearing of gold jewelry or fine clothes. Rather, it should be that of your inner self, the unfading beauty of a gentle and quiet spirit, which is of great worth in God's sight.

~1 Peter 3:3-4

Wedding Dresses

"Girls," said Mom. "Aunt Annette is here." Caitlin and Sierra, sisters, greeted their aunt at the door.

"Mom said you have good news," said Sierra. "Tell us!"

"I'm getting married!" said Aunt Annette. "And I want you and Caitlin to help with my wedding."

"Yay!" said Sierra, giving her aunt a hug.

"Congratulations!" said Caitlin. "When's the wedding?"

"Next month. I know that doesn't give you very much time to hunt for dresses."

"Whoa!" said Caitlin. "You mean I have to wear a dress? How about my nice, designer jeans and a beautiful shirt?"

"You and Sierra will run the gift table. That means you'll be taking gifts from guests at the door and placing them on the tables. I'd like you both in pretty dresses," said Aunt Annette.

"Fine," said Caitlin. "But I want to choose the dress."

"We'll choose together," said Mom.

"Well, I need to go finish wedding plans," said Aunt Annette. "Thanks, girls!"

"Bye, Aunt Annette," said Caitlin and Sierra. They walked into the kitchen to get a snack.

"This is so cool," said Sierra. "I've never been in a wedding. I can imagine sparkly dresses swishing around our legs."

"Keep imagining," said Caitlin. "You won't catch me in a swishy dress."

"Why not?" asked Sierra. "You're so pretty with your brown hair and hazel eyes."

"I'm comfortable in my riding clothes. You know I love riding my horse. I don't feel right in a dress. Besides, your shiny black hair makes you look good in any color," said Caitlin.

"My Chinese heritage does have its advantages," smiled Sierra. She munched on some apple slices and found the latest issue of *Girl Magazine*.

"Hey, Cait, here are some beautiful summer dresses."

"Not interested," said Caitlin. "I'm going out to the corral."

Mom walked in. "How about we go to the mall after supper?"

"Sounds great!" said Sierra. "What color dresses do you think we should look for?"

"Aunt Annette said her wedding colors are lavender and silver," said Mom.

"I'll go look online, too," said Sierra.

After a delicious supper of pot roast, Mom and the girls drove to the mall.

"I'll meet you in an hour, and you can show me some suitable dresses for Aunt Annette's wedding," said Mom.

In the first store Caitlin found a jean dress. "I wish I could wear this, but I don't think Aunt Annette would approve."

"Mom said the wedding colors are lavender and silver. Maybe we can find something purplish," said Sierra.

"Here's a purple dress. I'm going to try this on," said Caitlin. After a few minutes, she walked out of the dressing room.

"Umm, I think it's a little tight, isn't it? And it's too short," said Sierra.

"You sound like Mom," said Caitlin.

"I don't think it looks good on you. It makes you pale, and all I see is tight fabric."

"Oh, all right," said Caitlin. "Let's see if you can find something better."

The girls walked to another store. "Look at that sales clerk over there. She's beautiful. I bet she could help us," said Sierra.

The woman wore a miniskirt, blouse, and tons of make-up. "Could you help my sister and me find a dress?" asked Sierra. The woman glared at Sierra, looking her up and down with disdain.

"I guess," said the woman. "What kind of dress?"

"We're helping at a wedding and would like lavender dresses," said Sierra.

"Hmm. I might have lavender. Follow me."

They weaved in and out of the racks of clothes. Finally she held up two dresses.

"They are even on sale," said the woman, and then she left.

"She's not very kind," said Caitlin.

"She may be pretty, but she's ugly on the inside," said Sierra. "In fact, I just read about that yesterday in my devotion. It said that beauty comes from within."

"So do you like any of these dresses?" asked Caitlin. The first dress had ruffles, no straps, and was short. The second dress was a sleeveless dress with straps, knee-length, lavender with tiny silver sparkles scattered on the fabric. A satin belt with a circle diamond buckle accentuated the front.

"Let's try on the second dress," said Sierra.

"I agree," said Caitlin.

As they walked out of the dressing room, Mom greeted them.

"Beautiful," she said. "The dresses light up your faces. Aunt Annette will love them. You know girls, I'm proud of your decisions. You chose modest dresses that light up your eyes. That will bring glory to God!"

Mom paid for the dresses, and then they were treated to frozen yogurt.

What Do YOU Think?

1. What are some criteria or "rules" for choosing your clothes?

_____

_____

_____

2. Do you have a favorite dress or outfit? Describe it.

_____

_____

_____

3. What does it mean that beauty comes from within? Doesn't beauty describe how you look?

_____

_____

_____

_____

PUZZLE God's Beauty Secrets

Can you crack the secret code to find out five of God's beauty secrets?

Hint: Number the alphabet, with 1 being A and 2 being B, and so on.

___	___	___	___	___	___	___	___	___	___
3	15	13	16	1	19	19	9	15	14

___	___	___	___	___	___	___	___
11	9	14	4	14	5	19	19

___	___	___	___	___	___	___	___
8	21	13	9	12	9	20	25

___	___	___	___	___	___	___	___	___	___
7	5	14	20	12	5	14	5	19	19

___	___	___	___	___	___	___	___
16	1	20	9	5	14	3	5

Answer Key: These five beauty secrets come from Colossians 3:12.

1. Compassion – You want to help someone because you feel sadness for them.
2. Kindness – You show goodness to someone or bring them happiness.
3. Humility – You consider others better than yourself. You're not proud.
4. Gentleness – You show kindness and quietness, not being too hard.
5. Patience – You are calm in every situation. You don't complain or whine.

Fun Facts   Fashion of the Past

How did women and girls dress over 100 years ago? They were to remain ladylike and modest, wearing long dresses to the ground and not showing skin. If they went outdoors, they had to wear a hat; and some even wore long gloves.

With the war era (World War II), fashion changed as women had to work. Beautiful dresses gave way to uniforms and pants.

People debated about what women should wear when playing sports in the late 1800s. Could they wear a sweat suit or T-shirt with shorts? Absolutely

not! They hadn't been invented. A dress and hat were still in order! Some argued over the length of the skirt, especially for riding a bicycle. Imagine that! Today, just about any style goes as long as it's in good taste, appropriate for the occasion and you feel comfortable wearing it.

▷ Investigate:

Look through old photo albums of your grandma or great-grandma. How did they dress? How is their dress similar or different from today's styles?

Look in books or the Internet and find a photo or illustration of how women dressed 100 years ago.

Fashion Trends

Fashion trends have changed throughout the century. Can you match each era with its clothing description? You might need help from an adult or do research on the Internet.

_____ 1. 1900s-1920s

a. Tighter clothes, revival of the hippy look, neon colors, mixing clothing styles from eras before along with wearing whatever is comfortable.

_____2. 1930s-1950s

b. Miniskirts, bell-bottom pants, and tie-dyed shirts became the hippie look of those who were against the Vietnam War. Glittery fabric was popular, wearing lots of jewelry and looking preppy took place in the latter part of this period.

_____3. 1960s-1980s

c. Nylon stockings were invented during this era. Women recycled their old clothes into something new during the Great Depression time. Women started wearing pants as they worked while their men fought World War II. Actresses made poodle skirts popular in the latter part of this era.

_____4. 1990s-today

d. Women had dresses and hats for different times and activities of the day. The dress hem became shorter toward the latter part of this period.

See the answers on page 192.

ASK Anna

Dear Anna,

My friends make fun of the way I dress because I don't wear the right brand-named clothes or shoes. What should I do?

From: Ashamed

Dear Ashamed,

You have nothing to be ashamed about! If these so-called friends base their friendship with you on clothing, then I think you should look for better friends. Your clothes should glorify God. It doesn't need to be a brand name or the hottest fad. There are many ways to make your outfits beautiful without spending lots of money. You could find bargains at garage sales and thrift stores. For example, adding a fancy belt could make a shirt dressy.

Dear Anna,

My mom always makes me dress up for church, but my friend attends church in jeans and a T-shirt. Does God care how I dress?

From: Confused

Dear Confused,

God cares about your heart attitude when you worship. However, if a person dresses like a slob on purpose because of an uncaring attitude, then that is wrong. Before the Israelites could approach the tabernacle, they had to make themselves holy, usually by offering sacrifices and cleansing their bodies. God is holy, and He wanted His people to be holy, too. Today we can come before God with a clean heart, because Jesus died on the cross for our sins as our sacrifice. If we've confessed our sins to Him, we can worship Him with a clean, holy heart like the Israelites. This doesn't mean you should wear anything you want. You still have to obey your parents. And your clothing should attract people to Jesus.

· ·

Dear Anna,

As I grow older, I'm hearing a lot about dressing modestly. What does modest mean?

From: Curious

Dear Curious,

The dictionary says being modest is dressing decently and not showy. Usually, modest refers to how much skin is showing. You want to show respect to God and to others by covering up body parts that are private. If you're flaunting too much skin (chest or legs), others around you could feel uncomfortable. The same goes for tight clothing. Are people being drawn to Jesus or to your body?

· ·

Dear Anna,

Mom and I don't always have the same taste in clothes and shoes. For example, I want to wear some sandals with a little heel, but she thinks they're too grown-up. She said the heel isn't good for my back. What should I do?

From: Fashionista

Dear Fashionista,

Styles change each year, and your mom might have different tastes from you. But perhaps you can compromise. Share with her your likes and dislikes, but listen to her advice. After all, she knows what's best for you. Maybe you can find a shoe or clothing that you both like. And if it's expensive, offer to help pay for it from your allowance or savings.

God's View

Throughout the Bible, God made it clear that beauty doesn't come from what you wear. Expensive jewelry, clothing, hairstyles, and make-up are not what God looks at. He looks directly at your heart. The beginning of this chapter listed some qualities God seeks: compassion, kindness, humility, gentleness, patience, among many others. Do you have a heart of love for others? When they look at you, do people see a representative of Jesus Christ?

What do people think when they see the way you're dressed? Usually, the way you're dressed reflects how you act and feel. If you're all dressed up, then you act important and graceful. If you're dressed kind of sloppy, then you feel sloppy. How can you dress to attract people to Jesus? Show some effort in the way you dress and see how your attitude changes for God.

I also want the women to dress modestly, with decency and propriety, adorning themselves not with elaborate hairstyles or gold or pearls or expensive clothes, but with good deeds, appropriate for women who profess to worship God.
~ *1 Timothy 2:9-10*

Charm is deceptive, and beauty is fleeting; but a woman who fears the Lord is to be praised. ~ *Proverbs 31:30*

But the Lord said to Samuel, "Do not consider his appearance or his height, for I have rejected him. The Lord does not look at the things people look at. People look at the outward appearance, but the Lord looks at the heart." ~ *1 Samuel 16:7*

Trivia – Heavenly Fashion

Have you thought about what you will wear in heaven? Revelation 7:9 says there are multitudes of people from every nation wearing white robes and praising God. White is a symbol of purity. And since there is no sin in heaven, everything is pure. Heaven will be bright and glorious, reflecting the beauty and goodness of God.

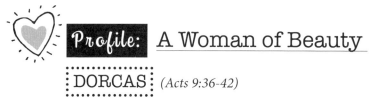

Profile: A Woman of Beauty

DORCAS *(Acts 9:36-42)*

Imagine yourself in a beautiful city on the Mediterranean Sea, a port for ships to come in and out with their goods for the people of Israel. Welcome to the ancient city of Joppa. The name Joppa means beauty! How fitting! In this city lived a woman who had just died from sickness. Her Jewish name was Tabitha, and her Greek name was Dorcas, which meant gazelle. A gazelle is a fast-running animal known for the beauty of its grace and ringed horn.

The apostle Peter preached in the nearby city of Lydda. When the Christians heard Peter was close by, they sent two men to bring Peter to see Dorcas. The custom in those days when someone died was to wash the body and wrap it in spices. They had placed Dorcas' body in an upstairs room.

When Peter arrived, he heard the wailing and crying of widows, Dorcas' friends. They showed him robes and clothes Dorcas had sewn for them. She had always gone about doing good and helping the poor. Peter sent everyone out of the room and dropped to his knees and prayed.

Then he said to Dorcas, "Tabitha, get up." She opened her eyes and sat up. Peter led her to the widows and the other Christians. Because of this miracle, people all over Joppa became believers in Jesus. Dorcas is an example of a woman with inner beauty of kindness, compassion, and humility. Instead of spending money on herself, she bought supplies to make clothing for widows. Dorcas not only knew about inner beauty, but she was concerned about the outer beauty of her friends. They were proud of the garments and showed them to Peter.

One of the most interesting facts about Dorcas' story in the Bible is how we meet Dorcas at her death. People had wonderful things to say about her. Dorcas' inner beauty sparkled long after she was gone. Do you have that kind of beauty?

Make it! T-shirt for a Friend

You may not be able to sew like Dorcas, but you can design a T-shirt for a friend.

What You Need:

* White T-shirt
* Fabric markers
* Cardboard

What To Do:

1. Think about the person you want to give the T-shirt to. What designs or drawings would look best? What colors look good on that person? What can you draw well? You could even include the reference to a favorite Bible verse.

2. Insert the cardboard inside the T-shirt to prevent the marker from bleeding through.

3. Carefully draw your design and image.

Surprise your friend with this special gift. If you have extra T-shirts, you can dress all your friends!

Fun Facts **Color Analysis**

If beauty comes from the inside, how can you show others what's in your heart? There's a popular saying that says, "The eyes are the windows to the soul." In other words, when people look into your eyes, they can usually tell how you're feeling. Did you know that you can choose clothes that enhance your eyes?

Color analysis is studying a person's natural hair, eye, and skin color combination. According to the combination, a person is labeled a season, such as winter, autumn, spring, or summer. Each season has a beautiful palette of various shades of colors that will make the person look fabulous.

Which season are you?

Let's try color analysis. Circle your correct answers.

Skin color: olive, brown, black, pale white, ivory, beige

Hair color: blond, brown, black, red

Eye color: blue, green, brown

*Now read the descriptions of each season and see which one matches your color combination.

Winter

Skin: pale white, olive

Hair: black, dark brown

Eyes: dark brown, blue, green

A winter girl can have olive skin with black or dark brown hair and dark brown eyes. Or a winter girl can have pale white skin, black hair, and blue or green eyes.

A winter girl looks great in deep, rich colors paired with bright white or icy pastels. Navy, dark brown, emerald green, fuchsia, royal blue, red, turquoise, black, white, and icy pastels are some of the colors that really stand out on you.

 # Summer

Skin: pale white, beige

Hair: ash blond, ash brown

Eyes: blue, green

A summer girl has ash brown hair with green or blue eyes.

A summer girl looks best in soft, dusty pastel colors. Mauve, lavender, plum, periwinkle, rose brown, and soft white are some of the colors that enhance your color combination.

Autumn

Skin: ivory, golden beige, dark beige, golden brown

Hair: red, blond, shades of brown

Eyes: green, brown

An autumn girl has many variations of hair and eye color.

An autumn girl looks great in earth tones and spice colors. Warm beige, warm gray, mahogany, brown, tan, lime, orange, and gold are some of your best colors.

Spring

Skin: ivory, golden beige, golden brown

Hair: red, blond, light brown

Eyes: blue, green

A spring girl should choose bright, lively, clear colors. Golden brown, creamy beige, shades of white, bright red, orange, purple, peach, salmon, true blue, navy, and yellow green will look awesome on you.

Which season best matches your color combination?

Look in your closet for some outfits in your palette of colors. Hold them to your face. Do you notice how your face brightens?

Make it! Barrette

Make a barrette in your seasonal color.

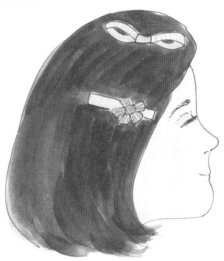

What You Need:

* Plain clip barrette
* 7 ½ inch ribbon—choose a color from your seasonal palette
* Scissors
* Craft glue
* Optional: tiny flower or sequin that matches the ribbon

What To Do:

1. You are going to line both the top and bottom pieces of the clip with a strip of ribbon lengthwise and glue it in place. You will wrap the ribbon around both pieces of the barrette clip lengthwise starting from inside the bottom piece then outside the bottom piece, then outside the top piece, and then inside the top.

2. Open the clip barrette and put a line of glue along the inside bottom of the clip. Lay the ribbon on the glue. Press it flat. Put another line of glue on the bottom outside of the barrette and wrap the ribbon smoothly on the glue.

3. Now put a line of glue on the top of the clip. Bring the ribbon up along the side of the clip and over the spring to the top. Lay it on the glue. Smooth it flat.

4. Open the clip, make a line of glue on the inside top. Continue laying

the ribbon on the glue. Cut the excess ribbon with the scissors. Let the glue dry.

5. If you have a flower, sequin, or other decorative item, glue it to the top. Allow time to dry.

Now you're set to wear your barrette. You could also make some for your friends.

:Memory Verse: Write the memory verse from the beginning of the chapter below. **(1 Peter 3:3-4)** Memorize it and recite it to someone in your family. How does this verse speak to you about beauty?

_____

_____

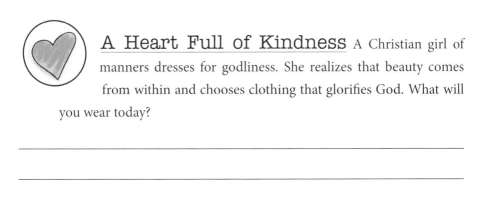

A Heart Full of Kindness A Christian girl of manners dresses for godliness. She realizes that beauty comes from within and chooses clothing that glorifies God. What will you wear today?

_____

_____

_____

Prayer Dear God, please help me to choose outfits that glorify You. I want people to see my heart of love for You. In Jesus' name, Amen.

Letters to **GOD.**

 ## Dear God,

The morning of Aunt Annette's wedding, Sierra, Mom, Aunt Annette, and I got our hair done at a salon. Aunt Annette loved our dress selection. To tell the truth, I liked the dress, too. Everyone said my eyes sparkled. The dress was comfortable and perfect for our job as gift table attendants.

Aunt Annette looked so beautiful in her white wedding dress. Maybe someday Sierra and I will wear a gorgeous wedding gown to our own weddings.

My eyes almost popped out of my head when I saw a girl wearing jeans and a T-shirt to the wedding. "No way!" said Sierra. And the girl was so loud, kind of rude, and obnoxious. Maybe it's true…what you wear is how you act.

You know, wearing a dress wasn't so bad. I guess the cowgirl in me leans toward jeans and a T-shirt. However, being dressed up today was fun. I felt important and happy that I could help my Aunt Annette. I learned that my clothes need to show that I love God and respect others. Maybe I'll wear swishy dresses more.

Good night!
Caitlin

Jot it Down!

Now it's your turn to journal about what you've learned about dressing for godliness. You can also write about how color analysis can help draw attention to your face.

_____

_____

_____

_____

_____

_____

_____

_____

_____

_____

_____

_____

_____

_____

_____

_____

_____

_____

✳ Chapter 5 ✳
Etiquette for Beginners

Show proper respect to everyone, love the family of believers,
fear God, honor the emperor. ~1 Peter 2:17

From Markers to Tea Cups

"Can I borrow your markers?" asked Zach, walking into Lexi's bedroom.

"Aren't you supposed to knock first?" asked Lexi. "No, you can't borrow them. You ruin my stuff. I'm doing my homework. Now get out of my room!!"

"You're a mean big sister," said Zach, as he let out a horrendous burp.

"Gross," said Lexi. "Now get out!"

Just as he closed Lexi's door, Mom walked in the house.

"All the flowers are watered and happy," she said. "Why did I just hear yelling?"

"Lexi won't share her markers with me," said Zach.

Mom knocked and opened Lexi's door. "I think you should share your markers with Zach. If something happens to them, he'll buy you new ones."

Lexi grabbed her marker box. "Here," she said with a scowl.

Zach made a face.

"Use your manners, Zach," said Mom.

"Thank you for the markers," he said with a half smile.

"While you're both standing here, I want to remind you that the pastor and his wife are coming over for supper. I hope you show them how much you love each other," said Mom. Zach went to his room.

"Little brothers are so disgusting," said Lexi.

"You must be kind to your brother," said Mom. "He loves you in his own way. Can you please clean up the living room for me?"

"But Mom, can't you see I have lots of homework?" Lexi whined.

When Lexi saw Mom's eyes, she obeyed. On the coffee table were candy wrappers, soda cans, toys, and newspapers.

"Why doesn't anyone clean up after themselves?" Lexi mumbled. She threw the trash away and hauled Zach's toys to his room. He was busy drawing when she walked in.

Lexi dumped his toys on the floor.

"Hey," said Zach. "Be careful with my toys."

"You shouldn't leave them all over the house," said Lexi. "If I find another one, I'll just vacuum it up."

"I'm going to tell Mom," said Zach.

Lexi left to vacuum the living room. When the house looked clean, Lexi worked on her math homework. But math wasn't her favorite. "I need Mom's help," she said.

Mom was on the telephone, so Lexi ate a banana while she waited. Mom was still on the phone, and Lexi really needed to finish her homework. She tapped Mom's shoulder.

"I need help," mouthed Lexi. Mom continued talking. Lexi found bubble gum and blew a huge bubble. POP! The noise startled Mom. Finally, she hung up the phone.

"Alexis Kay, you know you're not to interrupt my conversation," said Mom.

"I know, but I really need to finish this math," said Lexi. "I'm sorry." She chomped on her gum.

"Grandma was helping me with a recipe for tonight," said Mom. "After you finish your math, I'd like you to help me in the kitchen, please."

Lexi finished her math and then put on her apron. She helped Mom bake rolls and the lasagna. Then she set the table. Zach came in.

"I'll take out the trash," he said.

"Why, thank you," said Mom. "I love it when you volunteer."

"Now Lexi, when the pastor and his wife arrive, you can ask them what they'd like to drink," said Mom.

"How come everything has to be so proper?" asked Lexi.

"That's how I was brought up," said Mom. "Using manners shows respect, and knowing how to treat people is part of etiquette. In the olden days, a woman wasn't considered a proper lady if she didn't know how to treat others or host guests."

Lexi got out some teacups and a tray. She wondered if she'd be considered a proper lady when she was grown up. She decided to take mental notes from now on.

Ding-Dong! Lexi answered the door.

"Hello, Pastor and Mrs. Daniels."

"Hello," they both said, shaking Lexi's hand.

"What would you like to drink?" asked Lexi.

"Tea would be fine," said Mrs. Daniels. "I'll have water," said Pastor.

"Zach," yelled Mom. "Pastor is here."

Zach came out of his room and said hello. He accidentally bumped into Lexi. The drinks spilled all over her apron.

"I'm sorry," said Zach hurrying to wipe it up.

Lexi was about to scream at him until she remembered she wanted to act like a proper lady. "It's okay," she said. "It was just an accident."

Zach looked up at her in amazement. "You're not going to yell at me?"

"Nope," said Lexi. "I'm trying to be a lady."

Zach snickered.

"Did you know people can think badly of us because of our rude behavior?" asked Lexi. "Let's act like proper civilized kids. I'd die of embarrassment in front of the pastor if we fought."

"You're right," said Zach. "Here, I'll help you carry the drinks."

What Do YOU Think?

1. Can you name all the rude manners in this story?

_____

_____

_____

2. Who in your home is hard to get along with? Why?

_____

_____

_____

3. What manners are expected in your home?

_____

_____

_____

QUIZ "Do I Have Etiquette?"

How are your etiquette and manners? Do you know how to act in every situation? Take this quiz and find out.

1. When approaching a door, I ...
   a. walk through and don't look behind me.
   b. walk through, look behind me, and hold it open for the next person.
   c. walk quickly to be the first person through the doorway.

2. When I bump into someone, I ...
   a. pretend it never happened.
   b. say, "Excuse me."
   c. give the person a dirty look.

3. When I burp, sneeze, or pass gas, I ...
   a. pretend it never happened.
   b. say, "Excuse me."
   c. laugh and say, "Wasn't that a good one!"

4. When I want to use my sibling's things, I ...
   a. walk in his/her room and take them.
   b. ask before taking them.
   c. rip them out of his/her hands because I shared last time.

5. When I borrow my friend's game and it breaks, I ...
   a. keep it hidden and pretend I can't find it.
   b. apologize and offer to buy a new one.
   c. return it and say that I don't know how it broke.

6. If a bedroom door is closed in my house or a friend's house, I ...
    a. wait until someone else opens it.
    b. knock before opening it.
    c. open it and walk in.

7. When I'm eating at a friend's house, and I'm given a new food, I ...
    a. politely say that I don't eat this.
    b. eat it all without complaining.
    c. say, "What's this? I don't like this kind of food.
       Give me something else."

8. If I see someone new in my church group or at school, I ...
    a. stare at them and wonder who brought them.
    b. extend my hand to shake theirs and introduce myself.
    c. walk over to my circle of friends and ignore the newcomers.

9. If I'm invited to a birthday party, and I don't really like the person, I ...
    a. do not respond and ignore the person.
    b. tell the person I'm not coming and thank them anyway.
    c. tell the person I don't really like her.

10. I go with my friend's family to a baseball game. I address my friend's parents using ...
    a. sir and ma'am.
    b. their title and last names.
    c. their first names.

If you circled mostly A's, then you need to work on your etiquette. Take notes.

If you circled mostly B's, then you've been trained properly. Great job!

If you circled mostly C's, then you're a rude dude. Pay attention to this chapter.

Fun Facts

Bubble Gum – Etiquette

Since 1928, children have enjoyed chewing bubble gum. In fact, in 1994, the biggest bubble ever–23 inches in diameter–was blown in California. Bubble gum is fun to chew, but have you ever been around someone who chomped loudly or continually popped bubbles? Did you know there are rules for chewing gum? First, always chew with your lips closed. People don't like to hear your chomping. Second, don't blow bubbles in public. Third, when you eat or drink, always dispose of your gum and get a new piece. Don't save your gum for later. Remember to throw  your gum away properly in the trash. And last, don't chew gum when you're in the spotlight, such as giving a speech or singing.

Dear Anna,

My mom and grandma say that I need to learn etiquette. What is it?

From: A 5th Grader

Dear 5th Grader,

Etiquette is a way to behave in society. Etiquette is actually a French word that means ticket or sign. Etiquette started in the 1600-1700s under King Louis XIV in France. His gardener was tired of people walking across his nice lawns, and so he posted etiquettes or signs that meant to keep off the grass. In England, the Victorians wrote huge books of rules for everything, such as dressing, eating, bicycling, attending church, weddings, and funerals. Women had to study them. When the Pilgrims arrived in America, they left their etiquette behind. This prompted George Washington, at age 16, to copy the first etiquette rules for the new world in 1747. Living in America changed so much, and in 1922, Emily Post wrote a new book on etiquette. Since then, many others have taken on this opportunity to teach young people the art of fine living.

Dear Anna,

I thought etiquette was only for princesses. Why do I need to learn this?

From: the Un-Princess

Dear Un-Princess,

Let's get one thing straight. You might not be of human royalty, but you are of heavenly royalty. You are God's princess because He is the King of Kings! You may never greet the queen of England, but you can still act proper in society to draw attention to Jesus Christ.

Dear Anna,

My friend invited me over for a sleepover. I'm scared I'll say the wrong things or act the wrong way. What should I do?

From: Scaredy-Cat

Dear Scaredy-Cat,

Be sure to thank your friend's parents for letting you come over. Be yourself and remember your manners. (There's a list of manners later in this chapter.) If you're kind and thoughtful, I'm sure you'll have a great time.

Dear Anna,

My great-aunt died, and I'm going to her funeral. What's expected of me?

From: **Sad Niece**

Dear Sad Niece,

I'm sorry to hear your great-aunt passed away. And that's one of the first things you say to other relatives—expressing sympathy or showing you care. Many people send flowers, cards, or money. At some funerals there's a visitation before the funeral. That's when people come to the funeral home to visit with the family members of the deceased person. You would help greet the people and have pleasant conversation, often sharing memories of the one who died. They might even view the body of the deceased person. At the funeral, people used to only wear black, but now dark colors or anything respectable and conservative, not flashy and bright, is acceptable. After the funeral there might be a reception with refreshments for those who attended. Again, people share memories and eat. You could always help with the food, washing dishes, or just greeting people.

God's View

God's Word has plenty to say about how Christians should act. The whole Bible is God's code of conduct, or heavenly etiquette. If a person is rude and displaying bad manners, will that attract people to Jesus? Will they think the person is a Christian? Obviously not. Jesus said Christians are to be the salt and light of the earth. His followers should be the lily among thorns. In a rude society, Christians should stand out for their unselfish love. How did Jesus act when He was on the earth? He was a perfect example for us in how to love and show kindness. How can we tell people about God if we don't know how to act or treat others properly? In the New Testament, Paul taught Timothy, a young man, about etiquette. He taught him how to conduct himself as a leader in the church and to draw people to Jesus. Learning about social graces or manners and etiquette will allow you to show God's grace to your friends and family.

Don't let anyone look down on you because you are young, but set an example for the believers in speech, in conduct, in love, in faith, and in purity.
~ 1 Timothy 4:12

In the same way, let your light shine before others, that they may see your good deeds and glorify your Father in heaven. ~ Matthew 5:16

Like a lily among thorns is my darling among the young women.
~ Song of Songs 2:2

The entire law is fulfilled in keeping this one command: "Love your neighbor as yourself." ~ Galatians 5:14

Trivia – Communication Etiquette

There was a time when people communicated with one another by picking up the telephone, mailing a letter or simply talking in person. Etiquette for such communication was pretty simple: Say hello when answering the phone, start your letter with a greeting, and don't yell when talking to someone. Today, there are many more ways to communicate by using cyber technology—electronic communication networks and information technology. You are familiar with this technology through using a computer, the Internet, the World Wide Web, cell phones and video games. Here are a few cyber etiquette tips.

- When writing an e-mail, be clear and brief. It's not the same as talking in person.
- Only use terms, acronyms or emoticons that others will understand.
- Don't write anything bad about anyone. That would only encourage others to write something bad about you.
- When talking on a cell phone, don't talk too loud or too long. Let the other person have a chance to speak.
- Don't hog video game time. Share with friends and siblings.
- When playing games online with others, always be polite or they might not want to play with you again.

Profile: A Woman of Etiquette

LYDIA (Acts 16:11-15, 40)

If you were wealthy, what color would you wear the most of? Back in Bible days, purple signified you were rich and of a high position. Purple cloth was expensive because it was dyed from the juice of a lot of shellfish. The city of Thyatira was known for its purple cloth, and one of the dealers of purple from that city was Lydia. She was a high-class business woman and knew how to speak with important people. Most importantly, she worshipped God, but she hadn't received Jesus as her Savior yet.

On the scene enters Paul. He was determined to go to Asia to preach, but the

Holy Spirit prevented him and told him to go to Macedonia, a region of Greece. He sailed to the city of Philippi, a leading city, and found a place of prayer down by the river. A group of women had gathered, one of whom was Lydia. God opened Lydia's heart to respond to Paul's message about how Jesus had come as Savior. Lydia and her household believed and were baptized.

Lydia persuaded Paul and Silas to stay at her house. As a business woman who sold purple cloth, she was probably wealthy herself. She wanted to show hospitality and thankfulness for being lead to Jesus. On the way, Paul and Silas had some trouble and landed in jail for the night. However, God intervened, and an angel rescued them. The next day Paul and Silas headed straight for Lydia's house where they held a church service. Lydia's thoughtfulness and hospitality earned her a place in God's Word.

Try It! **12 Manners** <u>Everyone Should Know</u>

Place a check on the line if you display these manners:

____ Use "please" and "thank you" when I want something or receive something.

____ Never interrupt a conversation unless it's an emergency.

____ Say "Excuse me" after bodily functions, if I bump into someone, or if I need to get someone's attention.

____ If it's not mine, don't touch unless I have permission.

____ Knock before opening doors.

____ Don't use bad language.

____ Cover my mouth when I cough or sneeze.

____ Hold the door for people.

____ Don't make fun of people when texting or talking on the phone.

____ Send thank you notes for gifts I receive.

____ If I borrow something, return it in the same or better condition.

____ Be helpful. Don't whine or complain.

Make it! <u>Monogrammed Thank You Notes</u>

One important part of etiquette is to thank a person when you receive a gift. You might thank them in person, but it's still proper to send a thank you card. Fancy stationery has a person's monogram on the note card. A monogram is a combination of letters to form a symbol. Usually a monogram consists of your three initials. Your last name will be the biggest letter and in the middle. Your first name initial will be on the left side of the middle letter and smaller in size. Your middle initial will be on the right side of the middle letter and also smaller in size. So if your name is Tina Marie Cho, then your monogram will look like this: TCM. You can change the font of the letters to be fancy. Are you ready? Let's make your monogrammed thank you cards.

What You Need:

* Blank note cards from cardstock
* Glue stick
* Scissors and fancy-edged scrapbook scissors
* Ruler
* Patterned paper
* Solid color of cardstock that matches your patterned paper
* White paper
* Markers if you handwrite your initials, or a computer and printer if you print your initials

What To Do:

1. Measure a strip of patterned paper the same length as the note card and 1¼ inches wide. Glue it to the middle front of the note card.
2. If you're using a marker to make the monogram, cut a 1½ inch circle from white paper. In fancy letters, write your initials with a marker.

    If you're using a computer and printer, type your initials as listed above. Highlight the first letter and make it size 24 font (letter size). Highlight the middle letter and make it size 48 font. Highlight the last letter and make it size 24 font. You can highlight all three letters and choose a fancy font. Copy and paste this for as many cards as you want to make. Leave big spaces between each monogram to cut them out.

3. If you printed your monograms on the computer, then you'll need to cut them out in 1½ inch circles. Maybe you can find a circular item to help you trace.

4. Glue the monograms to the colored cardstock. Using fancy-edged scissors, cut around the circles to form a nice border.

5. Glue a monogram to the center of the patterned strip on the note card. Now you're ready to write a thank you note when you receive a gift or need to show appreciation!

 Memory Verse Write the memory verse from the beginning of the chapter below. **(1 Peter 2:1)** Memorize it and recite it to someone in your family. Do you think you treat everyone respectfully?

_____

_____

A Heart Full of Respect A Christian girl with manners knows social etiquette. She knows how to act, and she treats everyone with respect to draw them to Jesus.

Prayer Dear God, please help me to learn the proper way to act and treat others. I want to be a lily among thorns. In Jesus' name, Amen.

Letters to **GOD.**

Dear God,

Our supper with Pastor and Mrs. Daniels was terrific. Zach and I really surprised Mom. We didn't argue the whole evening and remembered our manners. Zach and I helped serve and even washed the dishes without complaining. Today a card came in the mail.

Dear Lexi and Zach,

We want to thank you for such a wonderful dinner. You two were terrific hosts and so polite. Your mother's lasagna was delicious, and the chocolate cake was heavenly. We look forward to seeing you in church this Sunday.

Smiles,

Pastor and Mrs. Daniels

I shared the thank you card with Zach and Mom. Zach and I have been nice to each other. We both feel that respecting each other makes life at home happier and peaceful. I try not to complain to Mom but to be helpful before she asks me to do things. For example, while I was playing catch in the backyard with Zach, I noticed more weeds in the flower beds and garden. I put on my gardening gloves and weeded. Boy was Mom surprised! She called me quite the young lady! It feels good to help others and be appreciated.

Good night!
Lexi

Jot it Down!

Now it's your turn to journal about what you've learned about etiquette and manners. You can also write about how you've shown politeness to your family and friends.

_____

_____

_____

_____

_____

_____

_____

_____

_____

_____

_____

_____

_____

_____

_____

_____

Chapter 6
Girl Talk

Do not let any unwholesome talk come out of your mouths, but only
what is helpful for building others up according to their needs, that it
may benefit those who listen. ~Ephesians 4:29

Abby's Birthday Party

"How do the streamers and balloons look, Abby?" asked Mom.

"The decorations look great. Thank you!"

"I want your 11th birthday to be special," said Mom. "I'm going to finish setting the table, and you can answer the door when your friends arrive."

Ding dong. "Hello, Sarah!" said Abby.

"Happy Birthday," said Sarah. "Here's your gift."

"Thanks. Come in and sit down."

Ding dong. "Happy Birthday, Abby!" said Grace.

"Thanks, Grace," said Abby. "Come in, and I'll take your coat."

"Sarah, this is my friend Grace from church. Grace, this is my friend Sarah from school," explained Abby.

"Nice to meet you," said Grace.

"Hi," said Sarah.

Ding dong. "That must be Candace," said Abby, getting the door.

"We found your house," said Candace. "Happy Birthday!"

"Thanks. Come in. I was just introducing everyone. Sarah and Grace, this is Candace, my friend from gymnastics class," said Abby.

"Hello, Candace," the girls said.

Ring-a-ling. Ring-a-ling. "That must be my cell phone," said Sarah. "Excuse me."

Sarah chatted on her phone in the hall while the girls snacked on some vegetables and dip.

"This is delicious," said Grace. "Did your mom make the dip?"

"Yes," said Abby. "She's a good cook."

Sarah returned. "You won't believe this. That was my best friend, and she said Philip got kicked off the soccer team because he got an F on his report card."

"Oh my goodness," said Abby. "Philip is the best soccer player our school has."

Ring-a-ling. Ring-a-ling. "That's probably my friend again. Hold on," said Sarah, grabbing her phone.

"I think she should turn her phone off," said Candace.

Ding dong. "Pizza's here," yelled Mom. She brought hot, steaming pizzas to the table.

"Yummy," said Grace.

"Eww, mushrooms and olives," said Candace. "I like Pizza School's pizza better."

"How long have you all known Abby?" asked Abby's mom.

"We've been going to church together for a couple of years," said Grace.

"Since kindergarten," mumbled Sarah, as she texted on her cell phone.

"Just a few months," said Candace. "Abby is an excellent gymnast."

"Thanks," said Abby. "You are, too."

"I used to take gymnastics," said Grace. "I was like five years old, and I remember learning how to do cartwheels and walking on the balance beam. The splits hurt my legs. Mom wanted me to be in a gymnastics meet, but I didn't want to. I wasn't that good. I really wanted to take ballet, but Mom insisted on gymnastics because  she'd taken gymnastics as a little girl. I had to attend …"

"Grace, stop rambling," said Candace. "We get it. You didn't like gymnastics."

"Sorry," said Grace. "I guess I get carried away sometimes."

"This new smart phone is just awesome," said Sarah. "Games, texting, e-mail, and face-to-face chatting keeps me so busy."

"Did you know you're at a birthday party?" asked Candace sarcastically. "I think you should turn your phone off."

"No way," said Sarah. "Abby, is it bothering you?"

"Well," hesitated Abby. "It's a little annoying."

"Fine," said Sarah. "I'll put it in my bag."

"Time to open gifts," said Mom.

"Open mine first," said Grace. She handed a small gift bag to Abby. Inside were earrings with a matching bracelet. "I made them."

"These are pretty. Thanks," said Abby.

"You're welcome," said Grace.

Candace whispered to Sarah, and they both snickered.

"What's so funny?" asked Grace.

"Candace said they're old-fashioned," said Sarah.

"I think you should be more tactful," said Grace. "You don't always have to express your opinions."

"I'm just telling the truth," said Candace. "I'm sorry if I hurt your feelings."

Abby opened Sarah's gift next—two T-shirts.

"I like these. Thanks," said Abby.

Candace handed Abby her present. "Colorful fingernail polish and nail stickers," said Abby. "Thank you! I love painting my nails. Hey, let's eat cake before we play a game."

Abby's mom scooped ice cream and cut chocolate cake. Abby gave each girl a pencil and a note pad. "This is for the game," she said. "Let's write a compliment about each person without signing your name. Then drop it into this container. I'll pull out a compliment, read it, and that person can guess who wrote it."

"Sounds like a dumb game," said Candace.

"It's fun," said Abby. "I've played it before. Give it a chance."

Abby turned on the radio while the girls wrote.

"Let's read our compliments and guess who wrote them," said Abby. The girls smiled as Abby pulled the notes out one by one and read them.

What Do YOU Think?

1. Describe the characters in this story.

_____

_____

2. If you were Abby, how would you get the girls to talk nicely to each other?

_____

_____

3. Think about conversations you've had today. What kind of positive or

negative talk did you use? _____

_____

_____

_____

Crossword Puzzle Word Power

Your words are powerful. They can make someone feel terrific or terrible. Can you match positive and negative conversation words from the Word Bank on page 106 with their meanings on page 107? Then place the words into the puzzle on page 106. (See the answers on page 192.)

Word Bank:

Complain   Compliment   Encourage

Gossip   Lie   Mumble

Ramble   Sarcasm   Swear

Tact   Tease   Thank

ACROSS

3. Not saying everything you think

5. Whine

9. To give hope

10. Make fun of someone

11. Opposite of truth

DOWN

1. To say the opposite of what you mean to with hurtful intent

2. Say bad words

3. Show appreciation

4. To say something nice about someone

6. Talk too softly

7. Saying bad things about someone

8. Talking too much

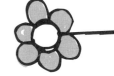

Fun Facts

Greetings in Other Cultures

In the United States, we often greet people by shaking their hands, smiling and saying hello. But other countries have different ways of greeting. In Japan and Korea, people bow and say hello. And in Korea, they don't call each other by first names. They call each other brother and sister. In Holland, close friends greet with three kisses on the cheek; first one cheek, then the other, and back to the first cheek. They also shake hands. And in Russian speaking countries, girls greet with one kiss on the cheek while guys greet with a handshake. Try it!

Saying Hello in Different Languages:

Japanese: Konnichiwa

French: Bonjour

Dutch: Hallo

Russian: Zdrazveetyet

Dear Anna,

I have some friends who keep saying "Oh my God" in a bad way. I know this is wrong. What can I say to them?

From: Concerned

Dear Concerned,

Using that expression is taking God's name in vain. Share with your friends that you worship God and ask them to please not use His name in a bad way. If they hear startling news, would they say, "Oh my and their own name?"

. . . .

Dear Anna,

I've sent text messages during church services, and some of my friends play games on their phones during the sermon. I don't feel this is right. What do you think?

From: Cell Phone Owner

Dear Cell Phone Owner,

You are correct. Using your cell phone for other than reading a Bible app is disrespectful because the person who is talking can see you're not paying attention. Would you want people to do that when you're talking? At church and other social functions, your cell phone should be turned off. That shows courtesy. And if you have to talk on your phone, you should leave the room.

Dear Anna,

When people give me a compliment, especially older people, I never know how to respond because I'm too shy. How should I respond?

From: Shy Girl

Dear Shy Girl,

The easiest way to respond is to just smile and say thank you. If you're feeling bold, then you could find something to compliment the other person about. For example, Mrs. X, I like your sweater.

God's View

Many girls have been blessed with the gift of gab. Girls love to talk! The Bible is chock full of verses about how to use our words. In James 3:6 the tongue is called a fire. It can destroy with just a few words. God's girls know how to be respectful in their speech. You're to build others up and encourage them. Most importantly, God wants you to share the gospel with others. Witnessing is the most important conversation you can have with someone. Do you know how to share God with others? First, tell what God means to you. Then you can share Bible verses and lead your friend to the Lord. If you don't feel comfortable with speaking in front of others, pray and ask God to help you. That's what Moses did! When God called Moses to lead the Israelites out of Egypt, Moses told God that he wasn't good at speaking. So God had Moses' brother Aaron, who was a good speaker, help him.

May these words of my mouth and this meditation of my heart be pleasing in your sight, LORD, my Rock and my Redeemer. ~ **Psalm 19:14**

Let your conversation be always full of grace, seasoned with salt, so that you may know how to answer everyone. ~ **Colossians 4:6**

You brood of vipers, how can you who are evil say anything good? For the mouth speaks what the heart is full of. A good man brings good things out of the good stored up in him, and an evil man brings evil things out of the evil stored up in him. ~ **Matthew 12:34-35**

My dear brothers and sisters, take note of this: Everyone should be quick to listen, slow to speak and slow to become angry. ~ **James 1:19**

Trivia From First Phone to First Cell Phone

The first phone call was made by Alexander Graham Bell, the inventor of the telephone, on March 10, 1876, to his assistant, Thomas A. Watson.

The first cell phone call was made by Martin Cooper, general manager of Motorola, on April 3, 1973, in New York. He had invented a 2 ½ pound cell phone. Cooper believed people should be able to take their phones anywhere, and he called it the personal telephone. Imagine the New Yorkers staring at him as he talked on a moveable phone while walking down the street. Cooper made his first call to the rival phone company, Bell Labs, to announce that he had beaten them in making a cell phone!

Profile: A Woman of Words

REBEKAH *(Genesis 24:1-66)*

Abraham's son Isaac was old enough to marry, and Abraham wanted his son to have a wife from his country and relatives rather than from among the heathen people of where he was living. Abraham sent his servant Eliezer along with ten camels and other servants and goods on the road back to his homeland to find a wife for Isaac.

How could Eliezer find the right woman for Isaac? While Eliezer's camels were resting by the well outside of town, he prayed to the God of his master Abraham. He asked God to let the girl for Isaac be one who came to draw water from the well and also showed kindness to him by watering his camels.

Before he even finished praying, God answered his request, and out came a girl with a jar on her shoulder! She went down to the spring and filled her jar. Eliezer met her and asked for some water. Instead of saying, "No, I don't even know you," she quickly lowered her jar for Eliezer to have a drink.

Not only that, the girl said, "I'll draw water for your camels, too." Remember, Eliezer had ten camels! She was gracious with her words. Back and forth she ran from the well to the trough, filling it with enough water for all the camels to be satisfied from their long trip.

Eliezer rewarded her with a gold nose ring and two bracelets. Finally, he asked who she was and if he could stay the night with her family. Rebekah was from Abraham's family on his brother's side. Eliezer realized God had answered his prayer, and he bowed to worship the Lord.

Rebekah ran to her home and showed them the jewelry, and her brother Laban greeted Eliezer and his caravan. Eliezer was so excited that before they ate he explained the whole story of how Abraham had sent him, and told about his own prayer to God for direction.

The next morning, Rebekah agreed to go with Eliezer and become a wife for Isaac. She and her maids left with the caravan. As they approached Abraham's home, Rebekah spotted Isaac in the field. Perhaps it was love at first sight! Soon they were married.

Make it! Scented Bean Bag

Make this scented bean bag to serve two purposes. First, you can use it to play Conversation Catch, which is explained next. Second, you can store it in a drawer to add a fresh scent.

What You Need:

* Two 4" x 4" squares of fabric, ironed
* Thread
* Needle
* Scissors
* Ruler
* Dried beans
* Essential oil in a scent you like such as lavender or vanilla

What To Do:

1. Thread the needle. (You might need help from a parent.) Line up the squares so that the pretty side of the fabric is facing inside.

2. Hand sew three sides in small, close stitches. Then pull the fabric inside out so that the pretty sides are on the outside. The seams should be inside.

3. Pour in dried beans. Add 3 drops of essential oil. Sew the last side. This seam will show on the outside.

 ## Play Conversation Catch

What You Need:

✳ 2 players and a bean bag

What To Do:

Practice your conversation skills by throwing and catching a bean bag. Practicing what to say will prepare you for when you really need to remember your speech skills. Say a line and then throw the bean bag to player 2. That person must reply and ask another question to keep the conversation flowing. Remember to smile, look each other in the eye, and use each other's names.

Conversation 1: Pretend you're meeting for the first time. Your conversation would go something like this.

Player 1: Hello. My name is _____. What's your name?

Player 2: Hi, _____. My name is _____. How are you today?

Player 1: I'm fine. How are you, _____? (Use their name)

Player 2: I'm doing great. It's nice to meet you. What did you do today?

…and the conversation can continue as long as you want.

Conversation 2: Pretend you're giving and receiving compliments at school.

Player 1: Your hair looks great, _____ (their name).

Player 2: Thank you, _____ (their name). I like your shirt. It brings out the color of your eyes.

Player 1: Thanks. How's your day going?

Player 2: It's going really well. What are you doing after school?

…and the conversation can continue or end.

Conversation 3: Pretend you're on the telephone.

Player 1: *Ring. Ring.* Hello?

Player 2: Hi, This is _____ (your name). Is _____ there?

Player 1: Sure. Please wait a moment while I get him/her.

(If the person isn't home, then offer to take a message.)

Make it! "Girls Talk" Board Game

With this board game, girls practice polite conversations and get to know each other better. (Boys and adults can play, too.)

What You Need:

* Sheet of paper
* 3" x 5" cards
* Pen
* Ruler
* Scissors
* Coins or buttons as tokens (2-6 players)
* 1 die
* 1 large plastic freezer bag with zipper
* Optional: stickers, cardboard

What To Do:

1. Use the ruler to draw a game board with squares on the sheet of paper. Or you can print one from the Internet by searching for a "free blank game board template." If you draw your own, first turn your paper the long way. Then make 24 squares along the border: 8 across the top and bottom and 4 along the sides.

2. Write START in the first square and FINISH in the last square. Write the following on different squares scattered throughout the game board:

   FREE SPACE (make 3)

   GO BACK TO START (make 2)

   LOSE A TURN (make 2)

PICK A CARD (on all the other squares)

3. For durability, you can glue the game board to a piece of cardboard.

4. Cut ten 3" x 5" cards in half. On each card, write the following topics:

- Tell about your most embarrassing moment.
- Tell about your scariest moment.
- Tell about your happiest moment.
- Tell about your saddest moment.
- Describe what makes you angry.
- Tell about your hobby.
- Give a compliment.
- Describe a pet you've had or one you wish you had.
- Tell about your favorite book without giving the ending away.
- Tell about your favorite movie without giving the ending away.
- Sing words to your favorite song.
- Give a compliment.
- Describe your best friend.
- Tell about a vacation or trip.
- What do you do in your spare time?
- Describe your favorite toy and why you like it.
- What is your favorite restaurant, and what do you eat there?
- Describe your favorite birthday gift.
- What would you like to be when you grow up? Why?
- How has God been good to you? Share.

5. You can decorate the game board and backs of the cards with stickers or designs.

6. Directions to play "Girls Talk" (You may want to print these directions on the back of your game board or another sheet of paper.)

- Select a token and place on the START space.
- Roll the die to see who starts first.
- On your turn, roll the die, read the message in the square. If you pick

a card, you must clearly answer the question on the card or do what the card says. Then return the card to the bottom of the pile. If you're unable, you must return the card to the bottom of the pile, and go back to START. If you receive a card you already had, you may exchange for the next card.

- If you land in a square with another token, you can send that person back to START.
- The first person to reach FINISH is the winner of "Girls Talk."

When finished with the game,
store the contents in a plastic freezer bag.

 Memory Verse Write the memory verse from the beginning of the chapter below. **(Ephesians 4:29)** Memorize it and recite it to someone in your family. How's your speech?

_____

_____

 A Heart Full of Kindness A Christian girl of manners can engage in a proper conversation. She speaks respectfully to everyone around her and shares God with them.

Prayer Dear God, please help me to speak respectfully to others. In Jesus' name, Amen.

 # Letters to **GOD.**

Dear God,

The girls really liked the game we played. It improved everyone's mood. Sarah's note said that she's caring, social, and good with technology. Grace's note said she's sweet, good at crafts, and a nice Christian. Candace's note said she's honest, a true friend, and leader. My note said I'm pretty, loveable, and hospitable. After the game we had a super chat with each other, and everyone was nice.

Since we don't all go to the same school, we decided to get together twice a month. We're starting a Conversations Club! Our next meeting will be at Candace's house, and we can invite one new friend who wants to participate in great conversation with other girls. The rules: no cell phones allowed, no boys, no gossip, no complaining, only say things that build others up. Grace might even bring a craft for us to do. In one of the meetings I get to share telling others about Jesus. I'm going to use the model of the Romans Road. These verses in Romans can explain salvation.

Romans 3:23 Everyone sins.

Romans 6:23 Eternal death is the punishment for sin. God provides eternal life as a gift.

Romans 5:8 Jesus' death paid the price for our sins because He loves us.

Romans 10:9 Believe in Jesus, that He died for your sins, to be saved.

Romans 10:13 Salvation is for anyone.

Good night!
Abby

Jot it Down!

Now it's your turn to write about what you've learned about the power of your words. You can also write about how you've used gracious words with family and friends.

_____

_____

_____

_____

_____

_____

_____

_____

_____

_____

_____

_____

_____

_____

_____

_____

Chapter 7
Table Manners

So whether you eat or drink or whatever you do,
do it all for the glory of God. ~ 1 Corinthians 10:31

Michelle's Fancy Christmas Dinner

"I'll wrap Grandma's Christmas present," said Michelle gathering a roll of pretty wrapping paper.

"Be very careful with Grandma's gift," said Mom. Michelle peeked inside the box. A beautiful china cup and saucer lay inside.

"Why does Grandma like collecting teacups?" asked Michelle.

"Remember I told you Grandma grew up in England and loves drinking tea," said Mom. "She has teacups from all over the world. Your dad brought this teacup from Russia on his business trip."

"I wonder how many teacups she has."

"Maybe you can count them while we're there," said Mom. Michelle cut the wrapping paper and taped up the sides. Then she added a huge bow to the top.

"Perfect!" she said. Michelle imagined Grandma in England drinking tea with the queen. Grandma liked being fancy. She had fancy dishes, a fancy house, a fancy car, and fancy clothes.

"Grandma is always fancy," said Michelle. "Sometimes I don't know how to act."

"Just behave and be yourself," said Mom. "I'll let you know if something needs fixing. Go put your Christmas dress on."

Michelle slipped on her red taffeta dress and slid the matching headband in her hair. "I hope I don't spill anything on this," she whispered.

"You look beautiful, honey," said Dad, kissing her cheek.

"Thanks," said Michelle. They put on their coats and drove to Grandma's house.

"Well, hello, Michelle!" said Grandma.

"Hello, Grandma," said Michelle giving her a hug. "Merry Christmas!"

"Hi, Michelle," said Aunt Melody and Uncle Doug. "You've grown so tall."

Michelle smiled. Grandma's house was decked out in red and green from the ceiling to the floor. A giant spruce tree stood by the window decorated with ornaments from all around the world. Michelle's gaze was fixed on the blinking lights.

"You can put your gifts under the tree," said Grandma.

"Oh yes," said Michelle, adding to the pile.

"Wash your hands, and you can help us in the kitchen," said Mom.

The smell of turkey made Michelle feel hungry. "Please help me put the silverware on the table," said Mom.

A red tablecloth and a poinsettia centerpiece covered the dining room table. Mom set china plates on each placemat.

"Can you please show me how to place the silverware?" asked Michelle.

"The knife and spoon go on the right side of the plate, and the forks and napkin on the left," said Mom. "Here, let me show you. We're using three forks tonight because we have a salad, turkey meal, and then dessert. So lay the napkin here, then the salad fork, entrée fork, and the dessert fork above the plate."

"How can you remember all this?" asked Michelle.

"I grew up living in this house," said Mom. "Grandma hosted many formal dinners."

Michelle completed one setting. "How's this?"

"Looks good," said Mom. Michelle finished setting the silverware in the correct spots.

"Michelle," said Grandma. "Would you like to make place cards? I already cut and folded the paper. You just need to write everyone's name."

"Okay, Grandma," said Michelle. Grandma handed her a marker. Very slowly and neatly, Michelle wrote everyone's name in cursive.

"Where do you want everyone to sit?" asked Michelle.

"How about you surprise us," said Grandma smiling. "Put the place card right above the dessert fork, dear," said Grandma.

Michelle set the place cards where she wanted them. Then Mom gave her the water pitcher. Michelle carefully poured water into everyone's glasses.

"Whoa," said Dad walking in. "Look at this grand table. Did you set this?" Michelle nodded.

"You'll be a proper hostess someday," said Dad. Michelle returned to the kitchen.

"The potatoes are fluffy and ready," announced Grandma. "Can you put this bowl of potatoes on the table, Michelle?"

"Sure, Grandma," said Michelle. She also carried the corn, rolls and butter, and salad to the dining table. Mom brought in the green bean casserole and turkey.

"It's time for Christmas dinner," shouted Grandma. "Michelle made place cards."

After everyone was seated, Dad prayed. Michelle laid her napkin in her lap just like Mom had taught her. Mom picked up the potato bowl and placed a scoop on her plate. Then she passed the bowl to the right to Michelle. Michelle took a scoop and passed the bowl. All the dishes were passed around the table. Michelle's plate was swimming with food.

"I hope you're hungry," said Dad.

"I am," said Michelle. "But I don't remember which fork to use first."

"Let's watch Mom and Grandma," said Dad.

Mom picked up her salad fork and ate a few bites of salad. Dad and Michelle did the same.

"Delicious, Grandma," said Michelle.

What Do YOU Think?

1. What kinds of problems do you have at mealtimes?

_____

_____

2. If you were Michelle, would you know how to set the table?
If so, who taught you?

_____

_____

3. What is your favorite meal, including dessert?

_____

_____

_____

 Quiz How Are Your Table Manners?

How do you feel when eating at a restaurant? Do you get confused about which fork to use? Take this table manners quiz and see if you have A+ table etiquette. Circle a letter to answer the questions below:

1. When eating soup, I should ...

    a. scoop the soup toward me and bring it to my mouth.

    b. scoop the soup away from me and bring it to my mouth.

    c. drink from the bowl.

2. If there is more than one fork or spoon, I should ...

    a. use the one closest to my plate first.

    b. use the one on the far outside of my plate first.

    c. use the longest one first.

3. When I'm eating with a group of people, I should ...

    a. wait for everyone to be seated.

    b. eat as soon as I get my food.

    c. wait for the host or parent to start eating.

4. While eating, my napkin goes ...

    a. on my lap.

    b. on the table.

    c. around my neck.

5. When I'm served steak or something that needs cutting, I should ...

    a. cut all the meat at once with my knife.

    b. cut one bite at a time with my knife.

    c. cut half of the meat with my knife.

6. If I have to go to the bathroom during a meal, I should ...

    a. leave quietly and lay my napkin on the table.

    b. announce that I'm going to the bathroom and lay my napkin beside my plate.

    c. say, "Excuse me, I'll be right back," and lay my napkin on my chair.

7. When eating with a group and food must be passed, I should ...

    a. put a serving on my plate and pass the food to the left.

    b. put a serving on my plate and pass the food to the right.

    c. help myself to all the dishes whenever I need.

Answers

1. b. In the United States, never drink from the bowl.

2. b. Always start from the outside and work your way in toward your plate.

3. c. Wait for the host or parent to start eating.

4. a. Your napkin can catch spills before they land on your clothes.

5. b. Just one bite at a time!

6. c. Say, "Excuse me," and put your napkin on your chair.

7. b. Always pass to the right.

   ✳ If you scored a perfect 7, you're fit to dine with the king and queen!

   ✳ If you scored 5 or more, you're comfortable at restaurants.

   ✳ If you scored 4 or below, pay close attention to this chapter and practice at home.

Fun Facts

Fork Confusion

Forks have been used since Ancient Egypt, Greece, and Rome. A fork is even mentioned in the Bible in 1 Samuel 2:13. However, forks during these days weren't used for eating. Forks with their long handles were used for lifting meat out of the pot. Noble people of the

Byzantine Empire (Turkey) started using the fork for eating, and in Italy people used the fork in the 11th century. The early fork had only two prongs or tines, and food kept slipping off. People in Europe were confused about how to use the fork. In North America, people were used to eating with their knife, spoon, and fingers or God's natural fork, as church clergy called it. Some churches banned the fork. Later, three to four tines were added to the fork, and by the 1850s, the fork became the preferred utensil. Now at fancy dinners we have up to three forks on the table—even more fork confusion!

Did you know chopsticks were used about 5,000 years ago, invented in China? In 500 A.D., the use of chopsticks spread to Japan, Korea, and Vietnam. Legend says people broke off twigs from trees to get their food out of big pots. Because of a big population and wanting to cook food quickly to conserve fuel, people cut the food into small pieces while cooking it. Therefore, knives were not needed at the table. Chopsticks became the

main utensil. Early Japanese chopsticks were made out of one piece of bamboo and connected at the top, sort of like tweezers. Later, they were split. Chopsticks were made mainly from bamboo, but the wealthy had chopsticks made out of jade, ivory, gold, and other metals. Each country uses a different-shaped chopstick as well. Some are flat, round, squared, or tapered. China, Japan, Korea, and Vietnam have their own way of setting the table with the chopsticks in a special place.

Dear Anna,

When I go to someone's house for a meal, I never know where to sit. I usually stand and wait for someone to tell me to sit. What's the proper way?

From: Guest

Dear Guest,

You're correct. When you're at someone else's house, wait for the host to tell you where to sit. Sometimes at fancy dinners, name place cards are on the table. Usually the host sits at the end of the table.

. . . .

Dear Anna,

I've heard of an appetizer or *hors d'oeuvre* and *entrée*. What do these words mean?

From: Foodie

Dear Foodie,

At fancy meals, there are usually five courses. The first food served is called an appetizer or *hors d'oeuvre* (or-durv) in French. This is something small like cheese and crackers. The *hors d'oeuvre* helps fill your tummy while you wait for guests to arrive or for dinner to be served. After you're seated, soup and salad are brought in. Fourth, the main course or *entrée* is eaten. This is your meat, vegetable, and pasta or rice. Last, dessert is enjoyed.

Dear Anna,

Is it ever acceptable to eat with my fingers?

From: Miss Tidy

Dear Miss Tidy,

Yes, some foods are meant to be eaten with your fingers such as the following: fried chicken, bread, grapes, cherries, carrot sticks, bacon, popcorn, chips, candy, and nuts. Of course, always wipe your hands on a napkin and never on your clothes! And licking your fingers is a big no-no.

Dear Anna,

It's so embarrassing when I get food stuck in my teeth. I just want to stick my finger in my mouth and get it out. I know that's impolite. What's the proper way?

From: Food-lover

Dear Food-lover,

You're right—you never stick your fingers in your mouth in public. The proper way would be to get a toothpick, go in the restroom, and pluck the food stuck in your teeth. If that's not possible, wait until you get home or somewhere private to brush and floss your teeth.

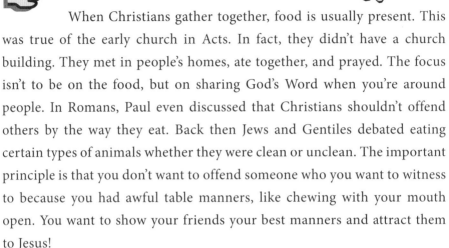

God's View

When Christians gather together, food is usually present. This was true of the early church in Acts. In fact, they didn't have a church building. They met in people's homes, ate together, and prayed. The focus isn't to be on the food, but on sharing God's Word when you're around people. In Romans, Paul even discussed that Christians shouldn't offend others by the way they eat. Back then Jews and Gentiles debated eating certain types of animals whether they were clean or unclean. The important principle is that you don't want to offend someone who you want to witness to because you had awful table manners, like chewing with your mouth open. You want to show your friends your best manners and attract them to Jesus!

They broke bread in their homes and ate together with glad and sincere hearts, praising God and enjoying the favor of all the people. ~ **Acts 2:46-47**

For the kingdom of God is not a matter of eating and drinking, but of righteousness, peace and joy in the Holy Spirit, because anyone who serves Christ in this way is pleasing to God and receives human approval. ~ **Romans 14:17-18**

Let him lead me to the banquet hall, and let his banner over me be love.
~ **Song of Songs 2:4**

When you enter a town and are welcomed, eat what is offered to you.
~ **Luke 10:8**

 ## Trivia Porcelain China

Have you ever wondered why fancy dishes are called china? Maybe your mom or grandma has a set. If you guessed that China is where they were invented, then you're correct! Porcelain was invented during the T'ang Dynasty (618-907 A.D.). Porcelain is made from a clay called kaolin. The Chinese could make beautiful porcelain. During the 13th-17th centuries, people in Europe and the Middle East wanted to buy and duplicate the china.

However, they failed until the 1700s, when England mastered the art of making porcelain similar to the Chinese. Now England is well-known for its quality china dishes.

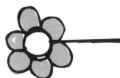

Try It! China Photo

Ask your parents or grandparents if they have china. If not, you can use your family's everyday dishes. Study the patterns and colors on the dishes. Many adults carefully choose the pattern for their dishes.

Other china sets are heirlooms, meaning they were handed down to your parents or grandparents from their parents. Look on the bottom to see if it says where the dishes were made. Take a picture of one of the pieces, print it, cut it out, and glue it into this frame.

Profile: A Woman of Hospitality

MARTHA *(Luke 9:38-42)*

What would you do if Jesus were coming to your house today? Clean? Cook? Get groceries? What do your parents do to prepare for guests? You can imagine the preparation involved when Martha found out Jesus was coming over! Mary, Martha, and Lazarus, who were sisters and brother, lived less than two miles from Jerusalem in the town of Bethany. Martha's name means lady of the house, and her name certainly fit her. The only thing on Martha's mind was having food prepared for Jesus, his disciples, and any guests tagging along to hear Him speak. She wanted to be a perfect hostess, serving food and making sure guests were comfortable and relaxed.

Close your eyes and picture the scene—a house big enough to fit all these people, Jesus front and center with people gathered all around Him, Martha busy preparing food in the kitchen, but wait—who is missing? Mary! Martha's sister Mary isn't in the kitchen or serving the guests food and drinks. She's sitting at the feet of Jesus. Martha is furious! Here she is doing all the work while her sister Mary gets to have fun listening to Jesus.

Well, Martha won't have it. She marches out to Jesus and says, "Lord, don't you care that my sister has left me to do the work by myself? Tell her to help me!" Perhaps Martha thought tattling to Jesus would make Mary embarrassed or make herself look good.

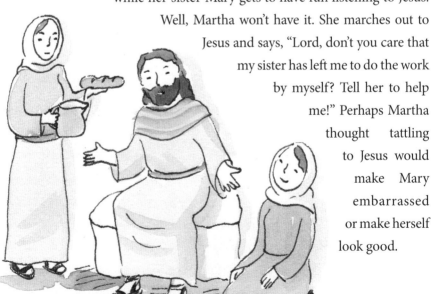

In any case, Jesus defended Mary and said, "Martha, Martha, you are worried and upset about many things, but few things are needed—or indeed only one. Mary has chosen what is better, and it will not be taken away from her."

What is more important, the food preparations or listening to Jesus? In John 11 we see that Jesus was very close to Martha, Mary, and Lazarus, and He loved them. Perhaps He visited them often and relaxed at their home. In spite of all the little details of etiquette, remember Martha's life and what's truly important.

Make it! Make Napkin Rings

In the 1800s, the dining room table settings became an art, a display of a family's wealth and standing. Often families used silver napkin rings to hold cloth napkins, as they had to reuse the same napkin until they were washed. Some napkin rings had each person's initials or monogram. You can make a set of pretty napkin rings for your family's table.

What You Need:

* Toilet paper tubes or paper towel tube
* Scissors
* Sharp knife *Have your parent help with this part.*
* Glue
* Ribbon or pretty paper
* Decorative items such as buttons or silk flowers

What To Do:

1. Cut the tubes into as many rings as you need. Have a parent use a sharp knife like a saw to cut the tubes into 1¾ inch rings.

2. Cut and glue ribbon or pretty paper around the rings.

3. Glue a decorative item to the top.

4. Roll up cloth or paper napkins and insert them inside the rings.

Try It! Prepare a Fancy Table Setting

Now it's your turn to practice what you've learned about table etiquette. You can cook a meal with your parents and set the table.

How to Set the Table

First, ask one of your parents if you have a table cloth. Cover the table with the cloth. You can also use placemats for each person. Now arrange the place settings.

Set the dinner plates in front of each person's chair.

The knife goes to the right of the plate with the blade facing toward the plate. To the right of the knife will be the spoon. To the left of the plate will be the fork. If you're using a salad fork and an entrée fork, then put the entrée fork next to the plate and the salad fork to the left of the entrée fork. The napkin with the pretty napkin ring goes on the left side of the fork, or you can place it on the plate if you're not using a soup bowl. The drinking glass goes above the knife and spoon. If you need a dessert fork, it goes above the plate, with the tines facing the glass. If you're serving soup, the bowl sits on the plate. If you're serving bread and butter, a small plate and butter knife go above the entrée fork.

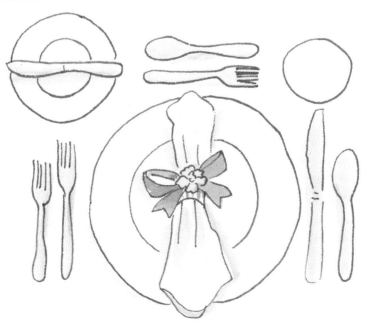

Whew! Step back and look at the table. Isn't it beautiful?

You can add a vase of flowers as a centerpiece, too.

Make it! Michelle's Pudding Pie

You can enjoy Michelle's favorite pudding pie using this easy recipe.

Ingredients:

* Graham cracker pie crust
* 1 box of pudding (any flavor)
* Milk
* 1 container of whipped cream or whipped topping
* Chocolate candy bar (optional)

What You Do:

1. Mix the pudding and milk according to the directions on the box for a pie filling.

2. Pour the pudding into the pie crust.

3. Put it in the refrigerator until set (firm).

4. Add whipped cream to the top of the pie.

5. If you used chocolate pudding, you can shave a chocolate candy bar using a vegetable peeler. Add the shavings to the top for decoration.

Memory Verse
Write the memory verse from the beginning of the chapter below. **(1 Corinthians 10:31)** Memorize it and recite it to someone in your family. How does family meal time bring glory to God?

_____

_____

 Letters to **GOD.**

 Dear God,

Dad and I survived the meal using all our silverware and table manners. For dessert Grandma brought out her fancy chocolate pie, my favorite! It had chocolate pudding on the bottom, topped with whipped cream and chocolate shavings on top of that. Mmm! I used a dessert fork for the first time that I could remember.

After dinner we opened presents. Grandma loved her new teacup. Of course, I counted all the teacups in her hutch. This new one is number 50. Grandma really surprised me with my gift. A small porcelain tea set. I can practice serving tea to my friends or stuffed animals.

The next day I asked Mom if I could set the table. I didn't want to forget what I learned. Mom fixed spaghetti, a salad, bread, and leftover pie. She even let me use her good china dishes. She had gotten them as wedding presents. I set candles on the table that matched the tablecloth. Dad was sure surprised to come home to such a fancy meal!

Mom said since I'm such a great hostess, we will invite missionaries over for a meal.

I'm going to make some other fancy napkin rings and look through Mom's cookbook.

Good night!
Michelle

Jot it Down!

Now it's your turn to write about what you've learned about table manners and etiquette. You can also write about how you've shown table manners and etiquette at your family meals.

A Heart Full of Grace A Christian girl full of grace uses proper table manners. She uses mealtime to attract people to Jesus and glorify God.

 **Prayer Dear God,** please help me to learn proper table manners. I want mealtime to glorify You. In Jesus' name, Amen.

Chapter 8
Etiquette on the Go

Even small children are known by their actions, so is their conduct really pure and upright? ~Proverbs 20:11

Out and About with Kristi and Jessica

"Thanks for letting me borrow your pencil," said Kristi.

"That's what friends are for," said Jessica.

"What are you going to do after school? It's Friday!"

"I don't think my mom has any plans," said Jessica.

"Would you like to come with my family to a play tonight at the community theater?" asked Kristi.

"Okay. But I have to ask my mom. I'll call her after class is dismissed," said Jessica.

The bell rang. "Goodbye, class," said the teacher.

Jessica called her mom on her cell phone. "Mom, may I go to Kristi's house? Her family is going to a play at the community theater, and then they'll bring me home."

Jessica turned to Kristi. "My mom said yes. Let's go!"

The girls ran to Kristi's bus. "Good afternoon, Mr. Baker," said Kristi, climbing aboard. "He's the nicest driver." The girls talked all the way to Kristi's house.

"Thanks for letting me come over," said Jessica to Kristi's mom.

"I'm glad Kristi has such a good friend. I have to run to the mall to pick up something, and we can eat dinner there, too."

"Jessica, this is my little brother, Ethan," said Kristi.

"Hi," said Ethan, playing with his cars.

As soon as Kristi's dad arrived, they drove to the mall. "Let's eat at the food court," said Kristi's mom. They ordered cheeseburgers, fries, and drinks. Kristi and Jessica sat at their own table. After Kristi prayed, they ate.

"Look at those boys at the table behind us," said Jessica. "They made a horrible mess. Napkins are everywhere, and they're dumping salt and pepper on the table."

"I think they left their manners at home," said Kristi.

"I bet they don't even have manners," laughed Jessica.

"Can I sit with you?" asked Ethan.

"Okay," said Kristi, "but you better behave." Ethan plopped down with the rest of his cheeseburger.

"Do you have any brothers or sisters?" Ethan asked Jessica.

"Oh my goodness," said Kristi. "Ethan, don't talk with food in your mouth."

"Sorry," said Ethan, still chomping.

After they finished, Kristi took their trays to the trash can. Ethan grabbed most of his trash, but he left his dirty napkins on the table.

"Don't forget your napkins," yelled Kristi.

"It's okay. The cleaning lady will get it," said Ethan.

"It's not okay," said Kristi. "You still need to clean up after yourself. What if everyone did that? Would you want to pick up after hundreds of customers?"

"I guess not," said Ethan, walking back to his table. They followed their parents into the mall.

Jessica sipped on her drink. "I'll wait here while you guys go into the store. I can't take my drink inside."

"I'll wait with you," said Kristi. "Oh, look. Here's a gumball machine. Ethan loves gumballs." She put in a quarter and a bright blue gumball rolled out.

"Here's a gumball for you," said Kristi to Ethan.

"Thanks," he said.

"I'm finished," said Kristi's mom. "Let's go to the play."

In the car Jessica asked, "What's the name of the play?"

"*Annie*," said Kristi.

"I saw the movie. I can't wait to see the play," said Jessica.

They pulled up to the theater. Kristi's dad purchased tickets.

"This is a beautiful place," said Jessica, checking out the big pillars and beautiful flowers.

"Our seats are this way," said Kristi's dad. "The play starts in five minutes."

Kristi and Jessica got programs and sat in the comfy theater seats. They were in a central balcony overlooking the stage.

"The view is excellent," said Jessica. Ethan sat between Kristi and his mom. Right at 7:00 p.m., the lights went out, and the stage curtains opened.

The narrator walked out and welcomed the audience.

All of a sudden, the silence in the balcony was broken with a POP! Everyone looked Ethan's way. A sheet of bubble gum was stuck across his face.

"You can't blow bubbles during a play," whispered Kristi. Ethan spit out his gum in his mom's tissue.

Once again they watched as young actors ran across the stage singing and dancing.

"This is really good," said Jessica.

"Yes!" said Kristi.

A small group of teenagers walked into the row in front of Kristi's family. "Excuse me," they said as they climbed over people's legs.

"I can't see," said Ethan.

"They're really late," said Jessica. "How rude."

Suddenly the audience started clapping. "I missed it," said Kristi. She, Jessica, and Ethan started clapping as well.

"When the audience claps, laughs, or is silent, we copy," said Kristi.

Ring. Ring. "Oh no," said Jessica. "I forgot to silence my cell phone." She quickly fumbled in her purse and shut off her phone; however, people still gave her ugly stares.

"Will we ever be able to enjoy the play without distractions?" asked Kristi.

What Do YOU Think?

1. Can you list the bad etiquette in this story?

_____

_____

_____

2. If you were the mom in this story, what conversation about manners would you have had with the children before entering the play?

_____

_____

_____

3. Have you ever been to a play or a concert? Which one? If you haven't been to one, which play or concert do you wish you could see? _____

_____

_____

_____

Word Search
Etiquette Is Everywhere!

Etiquette isn't just for you to use at home or with guests. You need to show etiquette everywhere you go. The hidden words on page 144 are places girls might visit. (See the answers on page 192)

C L S C H O O L A Z O O

M X W E R T Y I U O P K

A O T N A R U A T S E R

L K V X F H K T I Y R W

L G C B M L I B R A R Y

C H U R C H Y F K B C H

U H B R K P P A R K L D

W T I A F J Z V M R E O

K H F S Q W R Y G A M E

T H E A T E R E A T H L

M B C Z O L A K A L P Y

L A T I P S O H Y W P H

HIDDEN WORDS:

CHURCH   GAME   HOSPITAL   LIBRARY   MALL   PARK
PLAY   RESTAURANT   SCHOOL   THEATER

Fun Facts

How did plays begin?

Plays existed in Ancient Greece as a way of expressing religious beliefs toward their gods. The play was similar to a chant or hymn using actions and music. The words told about the adventures of the gods. Soon the words were written down, and a few actors were added. Later drama competitions were held, and wooden outdoor theaters were built. Instead of wearing costumes, the actors carried masks to show their facial expressions.

▷ Broadway

Today, the most extravagant plays and musicals occur on Broadway, a famous historical street in New York City. Around 40 theaters, famous actors, dazzling costumes and sets entertain visitors. It is an actor's highest honor to perform on Broadway. Maybe someday you can watch a Broadway musical, if you haven't already.

Dear Anna,

My friend has a wireless earpiece and microphone that lets her talk on her cell phone even when her hands are busy. It's pretty cool, but she keeps talking and ignores me, and it disrupts shoppers when we go to the mall. What can I do?

From: Concerned Friend

Dear Concerned Friend,

Sometimes it's hard to tell a friend something that will really help them, but it's for her own good. Try to get her to stop using her phone long enough to tell her that other people can totally hear what she is saying. Besides the fact that it's disruptive, she might not want others to hear her conversations. Let her know you value the times when she is talking to you directly. If that won't work, call her from your phone and tell her.

. . . .

Dear Anna,

I love watching sports games, but I'm disappointed when my friends are rude. How can I model good sports etiquette?

From: Sports Fan

Dear Sports Fan,

Watching a game is great fun, I agree. Make sure you and your friends know the game rules. Never boo or put down the other team. Be aware of those around you. If you're standing, make sure you're not blocking anyone's view, or immediately sit down. If someone is blocking your view, kindly say, "Excuse me, can you please sit down?" In the crowded stadium, never push or shove. Take your time and model how you want others to treat you. Be a good sport!

. . . .

Dear Anna,

My grandma is in the hospital, and I'm going to visit her with my family. Are there rules or manners I should know?

From: Granddaughter

Dear Granddaughter,

I'm sorry to hear your grandma is in the hospital. Yes, there are rules and manners you should observe in the hospital. Because patients need their sleep, you should be quiet in the hallways and hospital rooms. Always wash your hands before and after your visit to avoid spreading germs. Think of some interesting topics to talk about with your grandma. You want to encourage her and make her happy. Use your please and thank you's with the nurses and doctors. Stay out of their way when they come into your grandma's room for a check-up. You can be helpful by asking your grandma if she needs anything, like having her pillows fluffed, the TV channel changed, or more water. If she's in the hospital for many days, you could bring something to brighten her room such as flowers or balloons.

Dear Anna,

I'm attending my first wedding this weekend, and I'm not sure what to expect. I don't want to embarrass myself. Any tips?

From: Wedding Guest

Dear Wedding Guest,

Weddings are so much fun, enjoying a couple's happiness. Wear something nice. Usually girls wear a dress or very nice pantsuit. Your parents are probably taking a gift, but if you're attending without them, take a card and maybe buy a gift with your friend and split the cost. At the wedding, the spotlight is on the couple getting married. So never steal the attention of the crowd. Be respectful during the wedding ceremony, and at the reception remember your table manners. You might be introduced to a lot of new people. Smile and shake their hands.

God's View

God wants His children to have fellowship with other people. We're to get out, meet people, and share God's love with them. So it's great if you're able to go many places with your family and friends! However, people notice how you act, and this behavior eventually gets back to your parents. Jesus said we're to be a light to others in this dark world full of sin. We can spread the light of Jesus around through our behavior and good works. How do you want people to think of you? As that horrible-mannered child or as that wonderful Christian girl they love to be around?

In the same way, let your light shine before others, that they may see your good deeds and glorify your Father in heaven. ~ *Matthew 5:16*

Be completely humble and gentle; be patient, bearing with one another in love. Make every effort to keep the unity of the Spirit through the bond of peace. ~ *Ephesians 4:2-3*

Each of us should please our neighbors for their good, to build them up. ~ *Romans 15:2*

Make sure that nobody pays back wrong for wrong, but always strive to do what is good for each other and for everyone else. ~ *1 Thessalonians 5:15*

Quiz Out and About

How do you show manners and etiquette when you're out and about? Take this little quiz.

1. You're on the subway, and there's only one seat left. You and an old woman are standing next to it. You should ...

a. Sit quickly because you're younger.

b. Offer the seat to the grannie because she's older.

c. Do nothing.

2. You're cleaning out your dad's car and want to jam to some music. You should ...

a. Wear ear buds.

b. Blast your music.

c. Sing loudly.

3. You're on an airplane and spill your juice which splatters on the person next to you. You should ...

a. Pretend it didn't happen and get back to your movie.

b. Complain loudly about how clumsy you are.

c. Apologize sincerely and contact the flight attendant to help you clean up.

4. Your dog likes to go in your neighbor's yard and do his duty. You should ...

a. Clean it up.

b. Leave it there.

c. Keep your dog in your own yard.

5. You're at the library, and some people are being very loud. You should ...

a. Give them a dirty look.

b. Report them to the librarian.

c. Move to a quieter spot.

6. You fly to another country for vacation. You should ...

a. Stare at people speaking a different language.

b. Realize people have different customs.

c. Demand everything be the same as your country.

7. At school, someone next to you forgot her lunch. You should ...

a. Share your lunch.

b. Sit somewhere else.

c. Brag about how good your sandwich is.

8. At the restaurant you find a wallet in the seat. You should ...

a. Take all the money out and keep it.

b. Take the wallet home.

c. Turn the wallet in to the waitress.

9. At a restaurant, your meal isn't quite what you expected. You should ...

a. Complain loudly to the waiter and demand a discount.

b. Say nothing and eat the food because you chose it.

c. Trade with someone at your table for their meal.

10. At church someone next to you forgot their Bible. You should ...

a. Share yours with them.

b. Pretend you don't see them.

c. Ask them why they didn't bring their Bible.

▻ *Let's check your answers.*

1. b. Always offer your seat to someone older or in need like a pregnant woman.

2. a. Your neighbors will appreciate peace and quiet.

3. c. Always apologize and offer to pay for anything you damage.

4. a. or c. First, you should keep your dog in your yard, but if it does run to the neighbors, clean it up.

5. c. Move to a quieter spot. You wouldn't want someone to tattle on you, would you?

6. b. Realize that everything will be different. Certainly don't stare or laugh when you hear a different language or see new customs.

7. a. Definitely share your lunch or offer to buy the other person one.

8. c. Chances are, the owner of the wallet will be calling the restaurant looking for it.

9. b. Unless something is truly wrong, eat quietly without complaining.

10. a. Share your Bible. It's a good way to get to know someone else.

▻ *How did you do?*

- If you got 1-4 correct, keep reading and practicing manners and etiquette everywhere you go.

- If you got 5-7 correct, keep working! You're almost there when it comes to manners.

- If you got 8-10 correct, you rock! Your manners and etiquette are a shining example to others.

Profile: A Woman on-the-Go

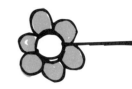

RUTH *(Ruth 1-4)*

During a famine in God's promised land, a Jewish family fled to Moab, and both sons married Moabite women, one named Ruth and the other named Orpah. Tragedy struck this family, and the father died. Ten years later, Naomi's sons also died.

Naomi heard good news from her homeland that God had provided food, and so she set off with her daughters-in-law on the road to Judah. Naomi must've had second thoughts because along the way she told Ruth and Orpah to return to their mothers' homes and remarry. However, both daughters-in-law wept and said they would go back with Naomi to her people. But again, Naomi urged them to go home. So Orpah took Naomi's advice, kissed her mother-in-law and returned. A third time Naomi told Ruth to leave, but Ruth clung by Naomi's side and said the famous words, "Where you go, I will go, and where you stay I will stay. Your people will be my people and your God my God …"

Naomi and Ruth arrived in Judah just in time for the barley harvest. Ruth was a perfect caretaker for Naomi and offered to go pick leftover grain in the fields. Ruth just happened to work in fields belonging to Boaz, one of Naomi's relatives. Ruth's kindness, manners, and etiquette made her stand out from all the other gleaners and even got the attention of the boss, Boaz! In fact, he asked who she was. He was so impressed with her that he told her to stay in his fields and work and

help herself to water, and told his workers to drop extra grain just for her. With this news, Ruth bowed with her face to the ground. And Boaz paid her another compliment. He'd been told about how she cared for her mother-in-law since the death of her own husband and how she left her own parents and homeland to live in a foreign country.

Naomi was quite surprised and happy to know Ruth worked in the fields of a relative. In this culture, because Naomi and Ruth were widows, a kinsman redeemer could rescue the family from debt and marry the widow. Since Boaz was a kinsman to Naomi, he was offered this responsibility. However, there was a closer relative than him. So the next morning at the town gate both kinsmen showed up to discuss the selling of Naomi's land. The closer kinsman said he'd redeem it until he heard the rest of the deal, to marry the widow, Ruth. So Boaz was happy to buy all Naomi's land and gain Ruth as his wife.

Naomi's friends praised her daughter-in-law by saying that Ruth loved her and was better than seven sons. Boaz and Ruth gave birth to a son named Obed. Obed was the grandfather of King David. Ruth was truly blessed for her wonderful testimony everywhere she went.

Try It! **Etiquette** Scavenger Hunt

You've learned so much about etiquette and manners. Can you spot great behavior happening in places you visit? Check off each item on the list when you observe it happening around you.

____ Someone opened the door for me or another person.

____ I heard someone say "please."

____ I heard someone say "thank you."

____ I saw someone silence or turn off their cell phone.

____ I saw someone put a napkin in their lap.

____ I saw a correct table setting.

____ I heard someone say "excuse me."

____ I heard someone give a compliment.

____ I observed someone chewing with their lips closed.

____ I heard someone answer their cell phone with polite manners.

____ I heard someone introduce new people.

____ I saw people shake hands.

____ Someone listened to me while making eye contact.

____ I observed someone sitting with poise.

____ I wrote or read a thank you card.

____ I saw someone cut their meat one piece at a time as they ate.

____ I observed someone chewing gum quietly.

____ I saw someone treat an older person with respect.

Memory Verse Write the memory verse from the beginning of the chapter below. **(Proverbs 20:11)** Memorize it and recite it to someone in your family. What do you think people say about your behavior?

_____

_____

_____

 Letters to **GOD.**

 Dear God,

After Jessica shut off her phone, things were pretty quiet until the intermission. One of the kids in the row behind us brought his drink into the auditorium. You guessed it. The drink spilled, and it got on my shoes and purse. I wanted to yell and bonk the kid with my purse. But I remembered my manners and thought about what Jesus would do. After the kid apologized, I kindly said, "That's ok. That's why drinks aren't allowed in the auditorium." Jessica was shocked that I didn't lose my cool. So were my parents.

The second half of the play went perfectly. We were able to watch the play without distractions. Dad took us out for ice cream afterwards. Jessica said this was one of her favorite Friday nights. She invited me to spend next Friday with her family. They plan to go boating on the lake. That sounds awesome!

I'm so thankful for a best friend like Jessica. Just think about all the places we can go together, especially as school is almost out for the summer! Look for me at the beach, mall, park, skating rink, church, library, theater, lake, and friends' homes.

Good night!
Kristi

Jot it Down!

Now it's your turn to write about how etiquette is displayed in public. You can also write about places you've been to, and how you've shown etiquette.

_____

_____

_____

_____

_____

_____

_____

_____

_____

_____

_____

_____

_____

_____

_____

_____

_____

A Heart Full of Kindness A Christian girl of manners behaves wherever she goes. She wants to be known as a lovely child of God.

 Prayer **Dear God,** please help me to act graciously wherever I go. I want to attract people to You. In Jesus' name, Amen.

Chapter 9
Organization is the Key

For God is not a God of disorder but of peace ...
~1 Corinthians 14:33

Ellie's Bedroom

"Ellie, look out the window," said Mom. "The lilacs have bloomed." Mom opened the window, and the fresh lilac scent wafted in.

"Today is the first day of spring," said Ellie looking at the calendar.

"You know what that means," said Mom. "Spring cleaning!"

"Oh no," said Ellie, thinking of all the piles in her room.

"Actually," said Mom, "I was thinking of redecorating your room. You're not six years old anymore. We can get rid of the little girl look and go for something more stylish. Any ideas, Ellie?"

"Not off the top of my head. I'll think about it."

"Well, think quickly, because I'm going to the home store tomorrow and can pick up a can of paint," said Mom.

"Okay," said Ellie. "I'm going to call my friend Lakeisha. She always has great ideas."

Ellie went to the kitchen and called her best friend.

"Lakeisha, I really need your help. Mom is in a spring cleaning mood and wants to totally redecorate my room, even paint the walls. You know how unorganized I am. Your room is perfectly clean, like a page from a magazine. Can you come over and help me clean?"

"Ellie, you know I'm your BFF. I'll do anything to help you. I'll be over in fifteen minutes," said Lakeisha.

Ellie went to her room to get a head start, but when she opened the door, she felt overwhelmed. Books, papers, candy wrappers, soda cans, clothes, crafts, stuffed animals, and hair accessories were everywhere.

Soon Lakeisha came to the rescue. "Hi, Ellie! You're right. You do need help."

"I'm drowning in my own stuff," said Ellie. "Where do I start?"

"Well, first, let's sort your things into piles. Hmmm … let's put all the books and magazines over here, stuffed animals on your bed, clothes by the closet, trash in the wastebasket, papers on your desk, and everything else in this pile. Oh, and if you want to get rid of something, put it by the door," said Lakeisha running out of breath.

For the next hour the girls shuffled through all of Ellie's things. Some piles were very large, like the clothes pile. "When was the last time you cleaned your room?" asked Lakeisha.

"I don't remember," said Ellie. "Maybe a month ago. Or two."

"If my room gets messy, it drives me crazy," said Lakeisha. "Now let's go through the clothes pile. If it's dirty, throw it in your hamper. If it doesn't fit, put it by the door. Otherwise, let's hang it in the closet or fold it in your drawer."

The girls worked out a system. Lakeisha held up a piece of clothing, inspected it, and told Ellie where to put it. Half of the clothes were put back into the closet or dresser. The other half went into the laundry. One shirt was thrown by the door because it was too small.

Ellie looked at her room. "I can actually see the carpet," she said smiling. "You're good!"

"Where do you put your books and magazines?" asked Lakeisha. "I don't see a bookshelf."

"Right. I don't have one," said Ellie. "That's why they're on my floor."

"Maybe we can make one," said Lakeisha. "Let's move on to the desk. I'll hold up a paper, and you tell me if you need to keep it."

Most of the papers were old school papers which Ellie tossed into the trash. She found some photos and put them into her desk drawer. Lakeisha also gathered a handful of pens, pencils, and markers and put them into a pile.

"Where can I put these?" she asked.

"I ran out of room in this pencil holder," said Ellie.

"No problem," said Lakeisha. "We can make a new one. Let's tackle the last pile...the weird things."

In the last pile, Ellie had some dice, hair accessories, craft items, pieces of a puzzle, fingernail polish, stickers, knickknacks, and a trophy.

"My mom always says that everything has a place," said Lakeisha. "Let's find where all these little things go."

Ellie carried the fingernail polish and hair accessories to the bathroom. She found the game and puzzle boxes for the dice and puzzle pieces. She put the stickers on her desk. After dusting the knickknacks and trophy, she carefully displayed them on her dresser.

"We can make a storage box for the craft supplies," said Lakeisha.

Knock. Knock. "It's Mom. I think I'm in the wrong room," she said as she glanced at the floor.

"Thanks to Lakeisha, my room is organized," said Ellie. "I just need to vacuum."

"Have you thought about what color you'd like for your walls?" asked Mom.

"I'd like a lavender bedroom like the lilacs outside," said Ellie. "And Lakeisha will help me make organizers for my room."

"Wonderful," said Mom.

What Do YOU Think?

1. Are you more like Ellie or Lakeisha? What cleaning tips would you give Ellie?

_____

_____

_____

2. Describe your bedroom.

_____

_____

_____

3. If you could redecorate your room, what color or theme would you choose?

Why? _____

_____

_____

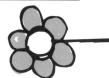

 Quiz Are you the Queen of Clean?

Read the description of each girl's bedroom. Circle the one most similar to yours.

1. All my clothes are put away, folded neatly or hanging in the closet. My bed is made. My dressers are neat, and the drawers are organized. The floor is picked up, swept or vacuumed. Wall hangings brighten my room.

2. Hangers? What are those? My clothes are everywhere. You can hardly see the floor. I never make my bed. What's the use? I'll be back in it soon. Wrappers and trash haven't made their way to the trash can yet. Books and toys are scattered about.

What kind of person are you?

If you circled #1, then you are the Queen of Clean!
You're a perfectionist, organized, and clean. You have a model bedroom. The queen could sleep here.

If you circled #2, then you're the Queen of Clutter.
You're slow to organize. Perhaps you're a social butterfly who'd rather be with friends than cleaning your room.

Fun Facts

Scrapbooking

What can you do with all your photos, cards, certificates, and special papers you want to keep organized? Have you ever tried scrapbooking? This hobby has become so popular in the United States that it even has a special day dedicated to it! The first Saturday in May is National Scrapbooking Day, which was established in 1994.

Long ago, there were no cameras or photographs. People arranged their precious cards, quotes, poems, and other mementos in a scrapbook. Even Thomas Jefferson clipped poems for his granddaughters and kept them in scrapbooks. And in 1872, Mark Twain, a famous American author, invented an adhesive scrapbook (prepasted pages). Now you can preserve your memories with this fun, creative hobby.

Make it! Pizza Box Scrapbook

You can make your own fancy scrapbook using a pizza box!

What You Need:

* 2 pieces of cardboard from a pizza box (if the bottom is greasy, use two pizza box tops)
* Scissors
* Glue
* Hole punch
* Fabric or heavy paper big enough to cover the cardboard
* 12" x 12" scrapbook paper
* 4 sheets of white paper
* 39 inches of twine or string

What You Do:

1. Trim the flaps off the top and bottom of the pizza box. You should be left with two flat square pieces of cardboard. Make sure the pieces are the same size.

2. Lay your fabric or big heavy paper on the table. Put one piece of cardboard on the fabric/paper so that there's a 1 inch border around the cardboard. Cut the fabric or paper.

3. Put glue on the plain side of the cardboard and press it onto the fabric or paper so that there's the 1 inch border all around. Now bend the 1 inch border flaps to the side of the pizza box with writing and glue them down. You may have to make little snips so that they lay flat.

4. Now you'll cover the pizza box writing by gluing the white paper so that it overlaps the flaps you just glued down. Now you've completed the top cover. Repeat steps 2-4 for the bottom cover.

5. Using the hole punch, make 3 holes, spreading them out at the top, middle, and bottom about an inch from the edge. Lay the punched cover on top of the other cover, trace the holes, and punch.

6. Arrange your scrapbook paper how you want it in your book. Punch holes.

7. Line up the bottom cover, scrapbook papers, and top cover. Cut three pieces of twine 13 inches long. Insert through the holes. You want to tie a loose bow so that you can open the book easily. To do this, ask someone to lay two fingers at the hole and then tie the bow. Try to open the book. Adjust the tie accordingly. Repeat for each hole.

8. Now you're ready to scrapbook! Add photos, stickers, and other pretty embellishments.

Dear Anna,

Not only is my bedroom messy, but my desk at school is, too! My teacher is always asking me to clean my desk. How can I keep it organized?

From: Messy Student

Dear Messy Student

Do you have different folders and notebooks for each subject? I suggest you keep your books on one side of your desk, and folders and notebooks on the other. Each time you get a paper, file it in the correct subject folder. Keep another folder for "Things to Finish" or "Do" and another folder for "Things to Take Home." Keep extra pencils, crayons, and markers in a pencil box. If you finish work ahead of others, use your spare minutes to straighten up your desk.

Dear Anna,

I want to redecorate my room, but my parents don't have extra money. What can I do?

From: Lil' Decorator

Dear Lil' Decorator,

There are many cheap ways to decorate. First, see what things you can reuse. You can always cover a box or add lace or ribbon to something. Usually garage sales and thrift stores are great places to find bargains. Ask your parents to take you on a shopping spree sometime without spending much money. Look through magazines for craft and decorating ideas.

Dear Anna,

Sometimes I go to my friend's house, but it's really messy. I feel uncomfortable. What should I do or say?

From: A Friend

Dear Friend,

You like this girl because of who she is. Don't let your surroundings bother you. If your friend's bedroom is messy, you could offer to help her clean it. Never put your friend or her family down. When you decide to meet, you could always offer to meet at your place.

Dear Anna,

My room is a disaster, and I know I should clean it. But when Mom asks me to clean, I just get so overwhelmed I want to cry.

From: Overwhelmed

Dear Overwhelmed,

A clean room is a healthy room. You don't want creatures (bugs) moving in because they see some great hiding places among your stuff. And you have a responsibility to take care of your things. To begin, take it slowly. Begin with one corner or one wall area of your room. Pick up only that area. I'm sure you'll see an improvement. Then the next day choose another corner area. After the floor is all picked up, try cleaning off a dresser, dusting it and arranging things nicely. Just clean a little at a time, and your room will look great in no time.

God's View

When God told Moses how to build the tabernacle and Noah how to build the ark, He gave very organized directions. God even instructed the Israelites how to live – from the smallest details, like what to do if mold started growing on their clothing or walls. God also gave detailed instructions in the New Testament on how to run a church. Our God is organized! And someday you will grow up and perhaps marry and be in charge of a home. God wants women to build up their homes and take care of them. Learning to be organized with your stuff means you're training for bigger responsibilities to come!

Then they can urge the younger women to love their husbands and children, to be self-controlled and pure, to be busy at home, to be kind. ~ **Titus 2:5**

The wise woman builds her house, but with her own hands the foolish one tears hers down. ~ **Proverbs 14:1**

She watches over the affairs of her household and does not eat the bread of idleness. ~ **Proverbs 31:27**

Whatever you do, work at it with all your heart, as working for the Lord, not for human masters. ~ **Colossians 3:23**

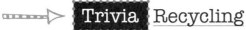

Trivia Recycling

Did you know you can help reduce waste by recycling some items? In 2010, Americans recycled 65 million tons of solid waste trash. This reduces air pollution by not having to make new raw materials. Before you throw a box or plastic item away, ask yourself if you can turn it into something useful to help you organize.

Try It! Cereal Box Magazine Holder

Recycle a cereal box to hold your magazines or papers.

What You Need:

* Empty cereal box
* Scissors
* Pen
* Contact paper or scrapbook paper
* Glue

What You Do:

1. Cut the top flaps off the cereal box.

2. On the skinny side of the box, cut five inches down along the edge from the top.

3. Using a straight edge, draw a straight line from the 5 inch point to the opposite top corner. You should see a triangle. Cut along this line. Repeat for the back of the box. Now your box is the right shape for holding magazines.

4. Cover your box with pretty paper or contact paper. Fold the excess paper inside the box.

5. Add a ribbon around the middle or add stickers. If you remember how to make the monogram from Chapter 5, you could make a monogram badge for the short side of your box.

Profile: An Organized Woman

DEBORAH: *(Judges 4-5)*

If you've ever watched a show or movie with a courtroom setting, you know what takes place is very organized. People have specific places to sit,

specific times in which to talk, while the judge oversees the proceedings. During this time in the Bible, a woman named Deborah was leading Israel as a judge. Israel lived in a cycle, beginning with sin, captured by the enemy, crying out to God, deliverance from the enemy through a judge, and then the cycle started over with sin. So for twenty years the Israelites had been oppressed by King Jabin of Caanan and his army commander, Sisera. God raised up Deborah as a prophetess and wife of Lapidoth. As a prophetess, she had a special understanding from God, and He helped her lead.

Deborah didn't have a fancy courtroom. Instead she judged from the Palm of Deborah, probably under palm trees. Perhaps she sat on a large rock and listened to the people's disputes and problems in an organized manner.

One day God revealed His plan to Deborah to have a man named Barak go with her to capture Sisera and his army. Deborah told Barak the very organized details of the plan: to take ten thousand men to Mt. Tabor while Deborah lured Sisera with his chariots and troops to the Kishon River where he would fall into Barak's hands.

However, Barak seemed scared and would only go if Deborah went with him all the way! Because of his cowardly attitude, Deborah said the victory would go to a woman. When Sisera found out Barak and his troops were headed up Mt. Tabor, he gathered his nine hundred chariots and men from the river. When Deborah sensed the timing was perfect, she said, "Go! This is the day the Lord has given Sisera into your hands." And Barak went down the mountain with his ten thousand men. God intervened, and Sisera's army abandoned their chariots and fled on foot. Every one of Sisera's soldiers died. However, Sisera escaped into the tent of a woman named Jael.

Jael invited him to rest, and she prepared a drink. He asked for water, but instead, she gave him milk and covered him up with a blanket. Do you know what milk can do to you if you're tired? It can help you sleep. While Sisera slept, Jael grabbed a tent peg and hammered it through Sisera's temple, or forehead, and he died.

Deborah's prophecy came true. Victory came by a woman. Deborah and Barak organized a song, called "The Song of Deborah." To compose poetry and any kind of music takes great skill, knowledge, and organization. God used Deborah to organize His people and set them on the path of deliverance.

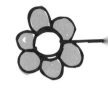

Make it! Scripture/Photo Wall Hanging

God wanted the Israelites to remember His words by posting them on the doorframes of their homes. In a similar way you can hang Bible verses throughout your home. Think of your favorite Bible verse or use one that became special to you from this book. Find a photo that would look great displayed on your wall with the verse.

What You Need:

* Bible verse
* 8″ x 10″ vertical picture frame
* 4″ x 6″ photo to go with the verse
* Glue stick
* 8 ½″ x 11″ sheet of scrapbook paper or 12″ x 12″ trimmed (Your wall hanging will look best if you use colors and patterns that match your room.)
* 1 sheet of white or colored paper for the verser
* Scissors
* Optional: ribbon, embellishments such as buttons or flowers

What You Do:

1. Look at your picture frame. Think about a layout, putting your photo toward the bottom and a Bible verse toward the top.

2. Trim your scrapbook paper to be 8 x 10 inches, to fit into the frame.

3. The Bible verse can be written or typed so that it fits onto a 6 x 4 inch white or colored paper, the same size as your photograph. Cut the paper to the correct size.

4. Glue the verse and photo onto the scrapbook paper, leaving space between the two and a border going around the edge. Be creative by adding embellishments such as ribbons, small flowers, or buttons.

Memory Verse Write the memory verse from the beginning of the chapter below. **(1 Corinthians 14:33)** Memorize it and recite it to someone in your family. How can you show you're organized?

_____

_____

_____

 A Heart Full of Kindness A Christian girl of manners has a welcoming attitude and room for her family and friends.

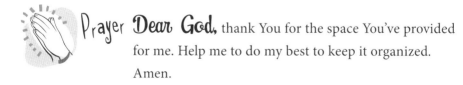 **Prayer Dear God,** thank You for the space You've provided for me. Help me to do my best to keep it organized. Amen.

 Letters to **GOD.**

 Dear God,

My room has completely changed. I helped Dad paint my walls lavender, and Mom pasted on a lilac wallpaper border. She even found some artificial lilacs and stuck them in a vase from the dollar store.

Best of all, Grandma surprised me with a lavender quilt that has flower designs and stripes along with matching pillows.

Lakeisha helped me reuse and recycle some items. We covered a vegetable can with contact paper and ribbon for my pencil holder. Then Lakeisha added purple lace to my white wastebasket. We found some baskets at garage sales, and tied purple bows on the handles. The large basket will hold my magazines. The smaller baskets will be for hair accessories and odds and ends. At the thrift store we found small picture frames. I put a photo of my family in one and Lakeisha and me in the other. Then I glued on some lilac flowers with purple ribbon in the corner. Mom said that wall hangings look good in groups of three. So I neatly wrote my favorite Bible verse on paper and glued it onto scrapbook paper. Again, I added some ribbon and lilac flowers to the corners and stuck it in another frame.

Wow! My room is so spring-like and clean. Oh, and one more thing, Mom bought a lavender air freshener. My room not only looks purple but smells like it, too!

Good night!
Ellie

Jot it Down!

Now it's your turn to journal about what you've learned about being organized. You can write how you've organized your own bedroom.

_____

_____

_____

_____

_____

_____

_____

_____

_____

_____

_____

_____

_____

_____

_____

_____

* Chapter 10 *
Proper as a Princess

Yet to all who receive him, to those who believed in his name, he gave the right to become children of God. ~John 1:12

A Princess Slumber Party

"Ella Clark, since you brought home a wonderful report card, you may have a slumber party," said Mom.

"Wow, thanks," said Ella. "I've never had a slumber party."

"It's like a sleepover at someone's house, except you can invite more girls, play games, and watch movies," said Mom. "You may invite four friends. Why don't you make invitations and choose a theme and food for your party?"

"I choose Alexis, Naomi, Victoria, and Kayla," said Ella. "Can Dad grill his yummy barbeque chicken?"

"Sounds great to me," said Mom. "You can write on their invitations that the party will be here at 6:00 P.M. next Friday night. Tell them to bring their sleeping bags, pillows, and clothing. Include your phone number on the invitations," said Mom.

Ella found some pretty paper, stickers, and scissors. She folded the paper to make cards, added princess stickers, and wrote, "You're Invited to a Princess Slumber Party!"

> **When:** Saturday, June 9th, 6:00 P.M.
> **Where:** Ella's house, 465 Orange St.
> **Bring:** sleeping bag, pillow, clothes, tiara
> **R.S.V.P.** 792-0393

Ella stuck the invitations into envelopes, addressed and stamped them, and slid them into the mailbox.

A few days later, Ella and her mother went to the party store. They found matching paper plates, cups, and napkins, and princess-themed balloons.

The day before the party, Ella's Mom said, "All of the girls have called to confirm that they're coming to your party."

"I can hardly wait!" said Ella. She went to her bedroom and made sure it was super clean.

An hour before the party, Ella set the table. She even made name place cards in the shape of crowns.

Finally, the clock struck 6:00. One by one the girls arrived. Ella placed their bags in her bedroom.

"While Dad grills the chicken, we can play volleyball," shouted Ella.

Alexis, Naomi, and Victoria were on one team, and Kayla and Ella made up the other team. Kayla served the ball, and Victoria blocked it.

The game was interrupted when Ella's dad yelled, "Time to eat!" After the girls washed, Ella's dad prayed.

"The table is so pretty," said Alexis.

"Yes, these name cards are cute," said Naomi.

"The chicken is delicious," said Victoria. Ella helped herself to potato salad, mac and cheese, corn on the cob, a roll, and Dad's famous BBQ chicken.

"And for dessert," said Ella's mom, "you can make a royal sundae." Vanilla ice cream, sprinkles, brownie bites, chocolate syrup, and candies lined the counter.

"This is awesome, Mrs. Clark," said Alexis.

"Thank you," said Ella's mom. "I want you to feel at home."

After everyone had loaded up on food and the dishes had been cleared away, Ella brought the girls to the living room.

"This isn't an ordinary slumber party," said Ella. "This is a princess slumber party. As princesses, we have to prepare to be proper ladies. We have a couple of games to play to show us how."

Ella had each girl put on their tiara.

"Princesses must walk with poise," said Ella's mom. "You want to walk elegantly with your head up high, like this."

Each girl copied. "Now let's take off our tiaras and let the real challenge begin. Who can walk correctly with the most books on their head?" Ella's mom asked.

The girls took turns. Ella made it with two books. Alexis and Victoria did three. Naomi did four, and Kayla did five. "Kayla is the winner!" She received a bracelet.

"For the next game, let's move to the kitchen," said Ella's mom. "As you get older, you must be able to set a table. In each bucket are utensils, a plate, napkin, and cup. Who can set the table correctly? On your mark, get set, go!"

Victoria's cup was on the left side instead of the right. Kaylas knife and spoon were switched. Alexis' napkin was on the wrong side.

"Naomi and Ella set the table correctly!" said Ella's mom. They both received pretty mugs.

"Before you watch a princess movie, why don't you change into your pajamas?" said Ella's mom.

The girls changed in Ella's room. "Nice jammies," said Naomi to Ella.

"Thanks, I like yours, too."

"Um, Ella, I forgot my pajamas," said Alexis. "Do you have some extra ones I could borrow?"

Ella froze. She had never loaned her clothes to anyone before.

"I g-g-guess so," she said, slowly digging out a pair. She remembered a verse she memorized about being kind to others. "Here you go," she said with a smile.

"Let's go watch the movie," said Ella to the group.

"Then we can stay up and tell stories," said Kayla.

What Do YOU Think?

1. Have you ever been to a slumber party before? If so, describe it.

_____

_____

2. What are your favorite games to play with friends?

_____

_____

3. If you could have a slumber party next week, who would you invite, and

what would be the theme? _____

_____

 Quiz Manners IQ Test

You're almost done with this book. Now you get to practice and show off all the great stuff you've learned. First, take this IQ test and see how close you are to being proper as a princess!

1. The book you've been waiting to read is finally in the bookstores. You buy one and leave it on your nightstand to read before bedtime. However, your little sibling beats you to it and leaves colorful drawings and signatures all over the book. A Christian girl of manners would:
    a. scream and beat up the little one.
    b. calmly say, "Please don't touch my stuff without asking. At least I can still read the words. Would you like me to read you a story?"
    c. get revenge.

2. Your cousins are coming for the weekend. You should:
    a. barricade your room.
    b. spend the night with your best friend.
    c. share your toys and anything else they need.

3. After a long day at school, you come home and:

    a. carefully sit on the couch, keeping your back straight and your legs to the side.

    b. plop on the couch, feet up, and lean on the arm rest.

    c. sprawl onto the floor while watching a movie.

4. Mom takes you on a shopping spree for a spring dress. You should:

    a. pick the latest style, no matter how long or short or how much skin shows.

    b. pick a modest dress that enhances your eyes.

    c. pick the most sparkling dress on the rack.

5. You receive a gift from your great aunt who buys you a toy that you're too old for. She hasn't seen you in ages. You should:

    a. call her and tell her that it's a baby toy.

    b. e-mail her a thank you, telling her that you liked the gift.

    c. write and mail a thank you card, telling her that you liked the gift.

6. You receive texts with gossip about your friend. You should:

    a. stick up for your friend by telling the sender not to talk badly about others.

    b. join in on the gossip and text other rumors.

    c. ignore the gossip and don't read the texts in the future.

7. You're invited to a friend's house for dinner. Oh no! You see lima beans on your plate. You should:

    a. tell your friend's mother that you don't like them and ask for something else.

    b. leave them on your plate and don't make a fuss.

    c. swallow them whole with a glass of milk.

8. You're at the park with some friends, a time to be yourself and relax. You're swinging on the swing and a little girl insists that she should get the swing.

You should:

    a. tell her "no way" because you were there first.

    b. wait for her to cry and then give her the swing.

    c. jump off and give her the swing because that's putting others first.

9. It's Saturday, and you know you're supposed to clean your room. But you get a headache just looking at all the piles of things on your floor and bed. Where do you start? You feel frustrated. You should:

    a. tackle one area at a time, and eventually your room will be clean.

    b. take an aspirin and have a nap.

    c. let clean-up wait until next week when your head feels better.

10. Most importantly, a Christian girl of manners should always:

    a. remember which fork to use.

    b. demonstrate proper behavior.

    c. never burp or pick her nose in public.

Answers:

1. b. The "old you" would probably pick one of the other choices. But to display manners, you must be patient!

2. c. Even though it might kill you to see your toys mistreated by younger cousins, you must share.

3. a. You must practice poise and good posture.

4. b. Your face is most important. Make it glow.

5. c. The proper way is to snail mail a thank you card.

6. a. Anyone would want you for a friend if you stick up for your pals!

7. b. This is actually correct. You don't want to make a fuss over your food.

8. c. Remember the golden rule.

9. a. Just work on a little at a time. A little goes a long way.

10. b. People remember your behavior. Are you a great example of a Christian girl?

Score

Give yourself 10 points for each correct answer.

What's your manners IQ? _____

100 **Hooray!** You're as proper as a princess.

60-90 **Keep trying**! You're almost there.

20-50 **You could use some more practice.** Keep doing the activities and review this book.

 **R.S.V.P.**

What does R.S.V.P. on an invitation mean? This French phrase stands for *répondez s'il vous plaît*. It simply means "please reply." People who host a party or a dinner need to know how many people are coming so that they can buy the right amount of food or reserve enough spots at a restaurant. When you receive an invitation, you might see R.S.V.P. Responding as soon as possible is courteous.

Dear Anna,

I'm having a birthday party next month, and I want to invite some school friends. Do you think it's okay to pass out invitations at school?

From: Birthday Girl

Dear Birthday Girl,

Passing out invitations at school does save money; however, if you don't have an invitation for everyone in your class, feelings can get hurt. If you do have an invitation for everyone in your class, then ask the teacher for permission or pass them out after school. You can also consider sending digital invitations if you have everyone's e-mail address.

Dear Anna,

I want to attend a sleepover at my friend's house, but I'm embarrassed to change in front of others. Should I just stay home or leave the party early?

From: Embarrassed

Dear Embarrassed,

Don't let that fear keep you from having fun with your friends. If you don't feel comfortable dressing in front of others, you can use the bathroom or ask to dress in another room. Keep in mind the other girls will be dressing also. So don't worry, they might have the same feelings about it as you.

. . . .

Dear Anna,

I want to wear makeup. My older friends wear it. But I don't think my mom will let me. What should I do?

From: Tween

Dear Tween,

Don't be in a hurry to grow up. Enjoy being a child. Makeup doesn't make you beautiful. Talk with your mom about when she thinks you're old enough to wear makeup. When the time is right, your mom might help you choose the right kind of makeup for your skin color. Remember, what's in your heart makes you beautiful!

. . . .

God's View

God tells us to offer hospitality to others. Hospitality is a friendly treatment of your guests. When people come to your home, are you kind? Do you offer them food and drinks? Do you share? The Bible lists many stories of people who offered hospitality to strangers, giving them food or a place to sleep. In 2 Kings 4:8-36, Elisha the prophet received hospitality from a couple who not only fed him, but they decided to make him his own bedroom so that whenever he passed through the area he had a place to stay. God honored their kindness by giving them a son. As a princess of the King of Kings, you can give others a royal treatment!

Share with the Lord's people who are in need. Practice hospitality.
~ Romans 12:13

Offer hospitality to one another without grumbling. ~ 1 Peter 4:9

For we are God's handiwork, created in Christ Jesus to do good works, which God prepared in advance for us to do. ~ Ephesians 2:10

Remind the people to be subject to rulers and authorities, to be obedient, to be ready to do whatever is good. ~ Titus 3:1

Trivia What do real princesses do?

Did you know there are still real princesses, queens, and kings today? Some of the countries that have princesses are Sweden, Norway, Denmark, Spain, Jordan, England, Japan, Monaco and Belgium. Most of these princesses have studied at universities, worked, and had children of their own. They support and raise money for charities (groups that help people in need). They might have royal duties such as traveling as a representative of their country. As one of God's princesses, you can represent the kingdom of heaven and do great works for God!

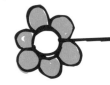

Profile: God's Princess

SARAH *(Genesis 12:1-5, 18:1-15, 21:1-7, 23:1-20)*

What would you do if God told your family to leave your country and relatives and go to a new land? This happened to Abram (age 75) and Sarai. God promised Abram he would become a great nation. Sarai obediently followed her husband; however, there were two problems. She was very old as well, and they had no children.

When Abram was ninety-nine years old, God appeared to him again and confirmed His promise. God changed Abram's name to Abraham, the father of many nations. Kings would come from Abraham's line. Sarai's name was changed to Sarah, meaning princess. She would be the mother of nations.

Just to make sure Abraham and Sarah understood that they would have a baby in their old age, God appeared to them again as visitors to Abraham's tent. Abraham hosted them and told Sarah to prepare some food. While she was in the tent cooking, God said through the visitors that next year around this time they would return, and Sarah would have a son. Sarah heard this and laughed to herself. But God knew everything and asked, "Why did Sarah laugh?" Even though they were very old, nothing would be too hard for God.

Abraham and Sarah had faith that God would do what He promised. Indeed, a year later, when Abraham was one hundred years old, Sarah gave birth to a son named Isaac, whose name means laughter. Sarah said, "God has brought me laugher, and everyone who hears about this will laugh with me." God was pleased with their faith, and both Abraham and Sarah's names were written in Hebrews 11:11 for believing that He'd fulfill His promise.

Sarah lived to be 127 years old. When Abraham bought land from the Hittites for her burial, the Hittites called Abraham a mighty prince. Abraham buried Princess Sarah in a cave on that land in Canaan.

 ## Try It! Plan a Party or Slumber Party

Now that you're an expert on etiquette, it's time to practice. Ask your parents if you can host a party or a slumber party. Decide on how many friends, the date and time, food, and theme.

The plans below are for a princess-themed slumber party, but you could easily adapt everything to fit your own theme. For games, you could try the same games that Ella used and even try some of the quizzes in this book on your friends! You could make crafts like bead jewelry or the God's Princess Catcher below. Another fun activity would be to have a pajama fashion show. Hand out awards for the most fun, creative, colorful, and unique jammies!

Party Planner:

Date of my party: _____

Time: _____

Theme: _____

Friends to invite: _____

_____

_____

_____

Menu: _____

_____

Games: _____

_____

Activities: _____

_____

✂ Make it! Crown Invitations

What You Need:

* Paper
* Scissors
* Markers
* Pencil
* Optional: jewel stickers

A Princess Slumber Party

What You Do:

1. Fold the paper in half. Place the fold near you. Draw a crown, using the bottom fold as the base of the crown. For a small invitation, draw the crown 4 inches along the bottom and 4 inches high.

2. Cut out the crown. It should open at the top.

3. On the front write "A Princess Slumber Party" or whatever the name of your party is. Color or add designs and stickers to the front.

4. Inside, write all the details:
   Who:
   Where:
   When:
   R.S.V.P.
   Your phone number
   Any items the girls would need to bring

You can put these invitations into envelopes and either mail or hand them out.

Miniature Crown Name Place Cards

What You Need:

* Cardstock or cardboard
* Scissors
* Pencil
* Marker

What You Do:

1. Fold your cardstock in half. This time you'll do the opposite of what you did for the invitation. Put the fold at the top. You'll need to draw the crown so that the paper opens at the bottom. Therefore, it's connected at the top by the "jewels."

2. Draw a crown 2 inches across and 1½ inches tall. Start by making the jewels at the folded top so that the fold is the top of the jewel. Draw the crown and cut it out. It should open at the bottom.

3. Write the name of your guest on the name card. Repeat for other guests.

 God's Princess Catchers

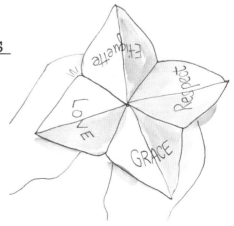

What You Need:

* Square origami paper
* Pen

What You Do:

1. Fold the square in half to make a triangle. Now open the square and fold it the other way to make another triangle. You should see an x fold.

2. Take a corner and fold it up to the center point. It forms a small triangle. Repeat with the other corners.

3. With the triangle folds down, flip the paper over. Repeat by folding up each corner to the center point.

4. Now fold the square in half. Open the square and fold it in half the other way with the triangle pieces inside.

5. Slide your thumbs and pointer finger under the square flaps and position the points all together so it looks like a flower. You should be able to open the catcher by moving your pointer fingers together upwards, which makes the catcher open like a beak, and then sideways.

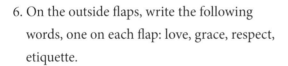

6. On the outside flaps, write the following words, one on each flap: love, grace, respect, etiquette.

On the inside triangles, write random numbers.

Open the triangle flaps and write messages and verses on the inner triangles such as: Share God's love. Your words are precious. You are God's princess! You're beautiful! You're graceful! What poise you have! You have the best manners. Be kind to one another.

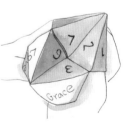

7. Now close it back up and have a friend pick an outside word. If the friend chose LOVE, then spell love by moving your catcher open and closed. Then wherever you landed, have your friend choose a number. Then count to that number by opening and closing the catcher. Repeat with a different number. Then have your guest choose one last number. Open up to the inner triangle and read her message.

Make it! Simple Punch

Princesses would love a frosty punch in a pretty glass with some cookies.

Ingredients:

* 2 two-liters of lemon-lime soda pop
* ½ gallon of sherbet (like orange or strawberry)

What You Do:

1. Place ½ gallon of sherbet in a huge bowl.

2. Pour the liters of soda over the sherbet. Slowly stir.

Share and enjoy!

Memory Verse: Write the memory verse from the beginning of the chapter below. **(John 1:12)** Memorize it and recite it to someone in your family. Are you a child of God?

_____

_____

A Heart Full of Kindness
A Christian girl of manners represents the King of Kings and extends hospitality to others.

Prayer Dear God, thank You for my friends. Help me to show them your grace and love. Amen.

Letters to **GOD.**

Dear God,

My slumber party was a blast! We watched a princess movie and ate pizza. Then we took off our tiaras and had a traditional pillow fight. Thankfully, pillows are soft! Honestly, it did take some getting used to seeing Alexis wearing my pajamas. As an only child, I'm not used to sharing. But she looked cute in my princess PJs.

Afterward, Kayla wanted everyone to tell stories. I don't like scary ghost stories, and so we made up a sentence story. I shared the first sentence, and then Kayla composed the second, Victoria the third, and so on. Our story was hilarious, about a frog prince! However, things turned ugly when Naomi started a new story and used real names from our class at school. I felt some of the sentences were gossip and put students down. So I tried to be brave and said, "This story isn't turning out nicely. I don't think our friends at school would appreciate it." My face turned as red as a tomato. I thought the girls would say angry words, but they said, "You're right, Ella. We wouldn't want them talking badly about us. We're sorry."

We ended up sleeping at 1 AM and woke up around 9 AM to a delicious breakfast of waffles. I gave my mom a big hug and told her thanks for the party.

Good night!

Ella

Jot it Down!

Now it's your turn to journal about a slumber party you've been to, or plan a future party here.

_____

_____

_____

_____

_____

_____

_____

_____

_____

_____

_____

_____

_____

_____

_____

_____

_____

_____

Puzzle Answers

Chapter 2, page 29 – Word Scramble

Answer key: 1. honor 2. value
3. praise 4. appreciate 5. admire
6. cheat 7. hurt 8. bully
9. ignore 10. selfish

Word for the verse: respect

Chapter 4, page 70 – Fashion Trends

d. 1. 1900s-1920s

c. 2. 1930s-1950s

b. 3. 1960s-1980s

a. 4. 1990s-today

Chapter 8, page 143 – Word Search

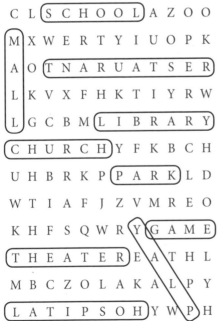

Chapter 6, page 106 – Word Power